PENGUIN ⦅🐧⦆ CLASSICS

THE ATHENIAN CONSTITUTION

ADVISORY EDITOR: BETTY RADICE

Aristotle was born in Stageira in 384 BC, in the dominion of the Macedonian kings. He studied in Athens under Plato, leaving on his death, and some time later became tutor to the young Alexander the Great. On Alexander's succession to the throne in 335 BC, Aristotle returned to Athens and established the Lyceum, where his vast erudition attracted a large number of scholars. After Alexander's death he was regarded in some quarters with suspicion, because he had been known as Alexander's friend. He was accused of impiety, and consequently fled to Chalcis in Euboea, where he died in the same year. His writings covered an extremely wide range of subjects, and fortunately many of them have survived. Among the most famous are the *Ethics* and the *Politics*. These have both been published in Penguin Classics.

●

P. J. Rhodes was born in London in 1940, and was educated at Queen Elizabeth's Grammar School, Barnet, and Wadham College, Oxford. He held a research scholarship at Merton College, Oxford, and worked also at the British School in Athens and Tübingen University. Since 1965 he has taught at Durham University, where he is now Professor of Ancient History; he has spent a year as Fellow of the Center for Hellenic Studies, Washington, D C. His main interest is in Greek politics and political institutions; his major *Commentary on the Aristotelian Athenaion Politeia* was published in 1981.

ARISTOTLE

THE ATHENIAN CONSTITUTION

TRANSLATED WITH INTRODUCTION AND NOTES BY
P. J. RHODES

PENGUIN BOOKS

PENGUIN BOOKS

Published by the Penguin Group
27 Wrights Lane w8 5tz, England
Viking Penguin Inc., 40 West 23rd Street, New York, New York 10010, USA
Penguin Books Australia Ltd, Ringwood, Victoria, Australia
Penguin Books Canada Ltd, 2801 John Street, Markham, Ontario, Canada l3r 1b4
Penguin Books (NZ) Ltd, 182–190 Wairau Road, Auckland 10, New Zealand

Penguin Books Ltd, Registered Offices: Harmondsworth, Middlesex, England

This translation first published 1984
Reprinted 1986, 1987

This translation, introduction and notes copyright © P. J. Rhodes, 1984
All rights reserved

Made and printed in Great Britain by
Richard Clay Ltd, Bungay, Suffolk
Filmset in Monophoto Sabon

CONTENTS

LIST OF ILLUSTRATIONS AND MAPS

INTRODUCTION

'An anonymous pupil of Aristotle' would not have looked attractive on the title page, and would have been awkward for purposes of reference; but although the *Athenian Constitution* was regarded in the ancient world as the work of Aristotle, and is accepted as such by some modern scholars, it was more probably written by an anonymous pupil and not by Aristotle himself. It is, however, a work of great importance. Classical Athens was the model of democracy in a world in which different city-states lived under different degrees of democracy or oligarchy, and in writing a study of the Athenian democracy – first a historical account showing how the classical form of the democracy had been brought into existence, and then an analysis of how the democratic constitution worked in his own day – the author has produced a work of a kind which no one had attempted until Aristotle set some of his pupils to study the constitutions of different Greek states.

Aristotle was born at Stagirus, in north-eastern Greece, in 384 BC. He was in Athens, as a pupil of Plato, from 367 until Plato's death in 347; he then left Athens, and after periods elsewhere was appointed by king Philip of Macedon to be tutor to his son, Alexander the Great. In 336 Alexander succeeded Philip, and in 335 Aristotle returned to Athens and opened a philosophical school there. In 323, on the death of Alexander, Athens embarked on a war against Macedon, and Aristotle left the city; in 322 he died, and Athens and her allies were defeated in the war; in 321 the democratic constitution of Athens was overthrown, at the insistence of the Macedonians.

Aristotle's *Nicomachean Ethics* ends with a transitional passage leading to his *Politics*, and towards the end of this passage he says (X. 1181b):

First, if any individual points have been well made by previous writers, let us try to follow them up; then from the collection of constitutions we must examine what sort of thing preserves and what sort of thing destroys cities and particular constitutions, and for what reasons some are well administered and others are not.

The corpus of Aristotle's works transmitted to us by medieval and renaissance scribes does not include a collection of constitutions, but there are lists of Aristotle's works made in antiquity, which mention far more than the surviving corpus, and which do include a collection of 158 constitutions. A man called Heraclides – probably Heraclides Lembus, who lived in Alexandria in the second century BC – produced a set of excerpts from the collection; later someone else produced a set of excerpts from the excerpts, which survived to be copied by medieval scribes: we have what amounts to a page or two of print on Athens (translated here on pp. 117–18), followed by much briefer passages on forty-three other states. Also we have references to and quotations from the collection by other ancient writers, and a collection of these 'fragments' made by V. Rose in 1886 filled 110 pages and ranged over sixty-eight or sixty-nine of the constitutions.

Meanwhile, in 1881, it had been suggested by T. Bergk that some fragments of papyrus acquired by the Egyptian Museum in Berlin two years earlier were from a text of the *Athenian Constitution*. Not everyone accepted the suggestion, and Bergk himself could not believe that a long quotation from a poem by Solon, in one of the fragments, belonged to the *Athenian Constitution*. Then, early in 1890, F. G. Kenyon, who was working on a set of papyri bought for the British Museum by E. A. T. W. Budge, identified as the *Athenian Constitution* a text written on the back of some abandoned financial accounts of the late 70s AD (and found that the Berlin fragments, including the quotation from Solon, did indeed belong to this work). The first public announcement was made in *The Times* on 19 January 1891, and Kenyon published the first edition of the text on 30 January 1891. Later a few separate, small fragments were found to belong to the British Museum's papyrus; but no other text of this work has been found, and no text of any of the other constitutions.

Some scholars had doubted Bergk's identification, and some

doubted whether the text published by Kenyon was in fact Aristotle's *Athenian Constitution*. Some of the doubts were quickly laid to rest: when the new text was compared with the quotations and references that were already known, it became certain that this is the work which the ancient world knew as Aristotle's *Athenian Constitution*. When the facts contained in the work were compared with what was known of Athenian history, it became certain (see pp. 31–2) that the work was written between 332 and 322, when Aristotle was alive and he and his school were in Athens. Nevertheless, there were those who maintained (and I believe that they were right to do so) that the work was written not by Aristotle himself but by one of his pupils.

Three reasons were given for denying that Aristotle himself was the author, the first a linguistic reason. Even in translation, it is immediately apparent that the *Athenian Constitution* is utterly different from the other extant works of Aristotle: the other works speculate about a series of problems, or generalize from a large number of particular instances, and are written in an idiosyncratic, highly condensed style; this work is an account of one instance, and is much more straightforward and readable in manner. The work does contain some Greek expressions which are characteristic of Aristotle, but a great many Aristotelian expressions which we might expect to find are absent, and there are remarkably few passages which have a strong Aristotelian flavour (9.2, the beginning of 26.2 and the end of 41.2 are the most markedly Aristotelian passages).

Secondly, the *Athenian Constitution* was compared with the *Politics*. The passage quoted on page 10 implies that the *Politics* is to be based on the collection of constitutions: it is hard to date the different parts of the *Politics*, but the latest certain allusion is to the murder of Philip of Macedon in 336 (V. 1311b), and the *Athenian Constitution* was not written until some years later. The *Athenian Constitution* does display the same general political outlook as the *Politics*: a liking for mild oligarchy and a dislike of extreme democracy. There are passages in the *Athenian Constitution* which closely resemble the *Politics*: 9.2, denying that Solon intended the democracy which was later built on his foundations (II. 1273b–1274a); 23–4, making the battle of Salamis responsible both for a more oligarchic regime under the leadership of the Areopagus and for the growth of Athenian naval power and the democracy (V. 1304a); and the remarks in 41.2 on the completion of the extreme democracy recall several passages in the *Politics*. However, there are also some notorious disagreements: chapter 4 gives us a 'Constitution of Draco', but the *Politics* says that Draco enacted laws for an already existing constitution (II. 1274b); chapter 8 says that in the appointment of magistrates Solon changed from election by the Areopagus to allotment from an elected short list, but the *Politics* says that Solon made no change in the method of election by the people (II. 1273b–1274a, III. 1281b). On account of these disagreements it was argued that the *Politics* and the *Athenian Constitution* could not be the work of the same man.

The third argument was based on the quality of the *Athenian Constitution*. It contains a great deal of valuable information which we do not find in any other ancient text, but it also contains a certain amount of rubbish. The 'Constitution of Draco' in chapter 4 is almost universally agreed to be a later forgery; in 26.1 Cimon is mentioned as a young man who had only recently entered public affairs, in a context of *c*.460 – when he was about fifty years old, had been active for twenty years, and had recently been ostracized. The author was not very skilful at reconciling conflicting material from different sources: 17.3–18.2, on the sons of Pisistratus, is badly confused and almost certainly arrives at some wrong conclusions; 23.3 puts Aristides and Themistocles on the same side in politics, but 28.2 seems to put them on opposite sides. Some scholars found it incredible that Aristotle should have been as incompetent as that.

In fact it is possible that, whatever his merits as a philosopher, Aristotle was not a very competent historian. Disagreements between the *Athenian Constitution* and the *Politics* prove nothing, because it is possible that on some points Aristotle changed his mind but did not bring his earlier writings up to date: the different parts of the *Politics* were based on the information which Aristotle had collected up to the time of writing, but he did not then stop collecting information, and if the *Athenian Constitution* was written later than the *Politics* that is not enough to prove that it was not written by Aristotle. The difference in style between the *Athenian Constitution* and the other works again proves nothing, because it is a totally different kind of work, and in particular is based on sources (and so likely to be influenced by their language) in a way in which the others are not.

There is, however, some force in the negative argument that there are very few passages which do recall Aristotle; and there is a further argument which can be based on the way in which Aristotle's school worked. Aristotle cannot himself have written all the many works with which he was credited: he can hardly have written all 158 constitutions. Aristotle was the first great collector of evidence, and he used his students as collectors: just as they were sent out to collect biological specimens, they were sent out to collect constitutions, and the 158 constitutions are the research projects of some of his students. Although he was in Athens when the *Athenian Constitution* was written, he was not an Athenian, and he was not an admirer of the Athenian democracy: there is no reason to think that he would have reserved Athens for himself. The ancient world attributed to Aristotle all the works produced by his school under his direction, but we are not obliged to do likewise: the *Athenian Constitution* should be recognized as the work of one of his students. Sometimes the student repeated things that his supervisor has said, or used his supervisor's language, and in his general political outlook he agreed with his supervisor, but occasionally as a result of his reading he disagreed with things that his supervisor had said.

The work consists of two parts, the first about twice as long as the second: a history of the Athenian constitution, and an account of how the constitution actually worked in the author's own day. It will be convenient to consider the two parts separately.

The first part runs to chapter 41 (the beginning of the work, equivalent in length to about five chapters, is missing from our text: the *Epitome of Heraclides*, translated on pp. 117–18, the author's own summary in 41.2, and one or two other allusions give us some idea of what was in it). The author's summary is the best guide to the purpose of the history: to list the changes which had taken place in the constitution until it had reached its present form. The history may be analysed as follows (the letters in the left-hand column refer to the sections into which I divide the translation, and the roman numerals and short headings on the right refer to the 'changes' of 41.2):

A	—	The lost beginning, from the foundation of the monarchy to the annual archonship	I Ion; II Theseus
B	1	Cylon	
C	2–4	Between Cylon and Solon	
	2	Causes of strife: poor enslaved to rich	
	3	Causes of strife: ancient constitution	
	4	Draco. (The 'Constitution of Draco' is a late insertion in the text, but I believe that the original text dealt with the ordinances of Draco.)	[Draco]
D	5–12	Solon	III Solon
	5	Solon's background	
	6	Shaking-off of Burdens	
	7–8	Laws and constitution	
	9	Solon and democracy	
	10	Measures, weights and coinage	
	11.1	Solon's travels	
	11.2–12	Solon in middle ground between two parties	

Aristotle believed that the *polis*, the city-state, exists 'by nature', and that man is a 'political animal', an animal suitable for the *polis* (*Politics* I. 1252b–1253a, III. 1278b); nature does nothing without a purpose (*Politics* I. 1253a, 1256b); so the works of nature can be analysed and explained, and human and political phenomena are works of nature which can be explained like any others (see *Movements of Animals* 703a, *Politics* IV. 1290b for the parallel between animal and state). He recognized four kinds of cause of the existence of any particular thing: the 'material' cause, the material from which the thing is made; the 'formal' cause, the form which the thing takes; the 'efficient' cause, the power that makes the thing; and the 'final' cause, the *telos*, the goal at which the thing is aiming (*Physics* II. 194b–195a). The constitution which developed in Athens was a democracy, and according to the analysis in Book III of the *Politics* democracy is not a 'straight' form of constitution but a 'perverted' form (1279a–b), so democracy cannot be conducive to the natural *telos* of the *polis*, which is the good life (1278b, 1280a–1281a); but, from another point of view, every form of constitution has its own *telos*, and the *telos* of democracy is freedom (*Rhetoric* I. 1366a). Fourth-century Athens was remarkably stable: after the revolutions of the late fifth century the democracy survived without any serious challenge, until it was overthrown in 321 not because of internal dissatisfaction but on the orders of Macedon; during that period there were many piecemeal adjustments, but there was nothing that could be regarded as a change of constitution. A man writing in the 330s and 320s could be pardoned for thinking that the Athenian constitution had by then reached the goal at which it had been aiming from the beginning; similarly, Aristotle writes in the *Poetics* that tragedy 'underwent many changes, but came to a halt when it had achieved its own nature' (1449a).

States can change their constitution for a variety of reasons, and they can change in more than one direction, so some of the changes listed in 41.2 take Athens further in the direction of democracy, but others interrupt that development. Ion's change (I) was probably regarded as an instance of progress; Theseus' change (II) certainly was, since it is described as a deviation from monarchy. (Draco is an intrusion into the original summary: see pp. 32–3.) Solon (III) provided the foundations of the later democracy; Pisistratus (IV), as tyrant, represents a setback; Cleisthenes' constitution (V) was 'much more democratic than that of Solon'. The ascendancy of the Areopagus (VI), the ancient council of ex-archons, marks an undemocratic phase; Aristides and Ephialtes (VII), weakening the Areopagus, resume the progress towards democracy, and what is said at this point about demagogues and naval power shows that the author includes the age of Pericles, treated in chapters 26–7, in this phase. Then follow the oligarchy of 411 (VIII); the restored democracy of 410 (IX); the oligarchy of 404–403 (X); and the restored democracy of 403 (XI). Here the summary ends – not because the author derived his history from a book written in the 390s, as some scholars supposed when the *Athenian Constitution* was first discovered, but because since then there had not been another change in the constitution: the democracy had persisted, and the author believed (in fact, wrongly) that it had continually become ever more extreme.

There are not many signs of political theory in this history. The idea of progress towards a goal (*telos*), underlying it but not expressed in it, is Aristotelian; comments in 26.2 and 41.2 echo remarks in Aristotle's *Politics*. The author disapproves of extreme democracy, like Aristotle and like most intellectuals in fourth-century Athens, but this does not invariably lead him to present democratic characters unfavourably: there is no criticism of Solon, and he is praised in 9.2 through a denial that he intended the extreme democracy which was later built on his foundations; Cleisthenes was more democratic than Solon, but there is no criticism of him; chapter 25 gives a favourable account of Ephialtes' reform of the Areopagus, and 26.1 is critical of the aristocratic Cimon. Studies which have claimed to detect a pervasive influence of Aristotelian theory are unconvincing.

How the author set about compiling his history, and what sources he used, have been endlessly debated. He quotes poems, particularly the poems of Solon (chapters 5, 12); on the revolutions of the late fifth century he quotes documents (30–31, 39). Much of what he says about the tyranny (14–15, 19), and the beginning of what he says about Cleisthenes (20.1–3), we can see are derived from Herodotus, and 14.4 refers to Herodotus by name. On the murder of Hipparchus (17–18), and on the revolutions of 411 (29–33), Thucydides seems to have been used, but on some matters our author disagrees with him, and at one point (18.4) he directly contradicts

Thucydides (but without naming him). Most of his material, how-ever, does not come from earlier texts which have survived for us to read.

There has been a tendency to think that our author was a lazy student and did not consult very many books, and that most of his history is derived from a single main source. Some scholars supposed that this source was a work of oligarchic bias written in the 390s, to explain why the history ends with the restoration of 403 (see p. 18); but the favourite candidate has been Androtion, active in the middle of the fourth century, and one of the series of Atthidographers (men who wrote an *Atthis*, a history of Athens). A minority of scholars have seen that some awkward passages in the *Athenian Constitution* result from the author's trying to combine conflicting data from different sources, and have realized that the theory of one main source fails to account for this: instead they have tried to classify the material in the work according to its nature and political slant. This is a better approach, but it may still be too simple to assume that all democratically inclined material comes from one source and all oligarchically inclined from another, and to substitute two or three main sources for one; recent studies on these lines have suggested that the author did not use even Herodotus and Thucydides directly, but based his history almost entirely on two or three *Atthides*.

I am prepared to assume that our author read rather more widely. He used Herodotus and Thucydides where they provided relevant material, on the tyranny, on Cleisthenes and on the revolutions of 411. The *Atthides* were an obvious source of material, and he used them in several places (his chronology probably comes from these works, and we can be fairly sure that at least what he says about ostracism in chapter 22 is derived from the *Atthis* of Androtion). There were other histories of a more tendentious kind: Stesimbrotus of Thasos wrote at the end of the fifth century about Athenian politi-cians; and Theopompus of Chios wrote in the fourth century, possibly but not certainly earlier than the *Athenian Constitution*, a work which was centred on Philip of Macedon but included two digressions on Athens; both of these writers were hostile to the democracy. We know also that a good deal of openly partisan writing was produced in the late fifth and fourth centuries: law-court speeches, and polemical pamphlets (for instance, the anti-democratic *Athenian*

Constitution which has survived with the works of Xenophon). Some of the material in our work, such as the list in 24.3 of all the Athenians who could be maintained at the expense of the allies, is probably derived from sources of this kind rather than from sober histories.

Not every sentence is necessarily based on a written source: occasionally our author may simply have written down what he thought he knew, without bothering to check his facts, as in the brief and inaccurate passage in 34.1 on the period between the end of the first oligarchy and the beginning of the second; he may have inserted the drinking-songs in 19.3 and 20.5 from his own knowledge. However, he probably did not do extensive original research: the fact that the *Athenian Constitution* and Plutarch's life of *Solon* overlap to a considerable extent, but not entirely, in their account of Solon and in their quotations from his poems suggests that they both made use of the same earlier account which already included quotations from the poems; at the end of the fifth century the restored democracy is not likely to have preserved oligarchic documents in the archives, and our author probably found these documents not in the archives but in a work which quoted them to show how innocent the intentions of the oligarchs had been. His opinions, too, are often second-hand: the verdict on the intermediate regime of 411–410 at the end of 33.2 is based on Thucydides (VIII.97), though given a slightly different slant. This is not to say that he did not believe what he said; but when he expressed an opinion it was not his spontaneous reaction to what he had found as bare fact, but a comment which he found in his source and repeated with approval.

Apart from Solon, and the one mention of Herodotus, our author does not name his sources. Several times he refers to a disagreement between the sources: this is always on issues which for him are marginal, and there are more important issues where we can see that he disagrees with an earlier text available to us but he says nothing of any disagreement. When he does mention a disagreement, he usually refers to the different sources simply as 'some' and 'others', but there are three passages in which he characterizes the sources. In 6.2–3 alternative versions of a story about Solon are attributed to 'democrats' and 'hostile sources': the democratic version is preferred, as more consistent with Solon's upright character, but there is no suggestion that the story may be wholly untrue (as it probably is). In 18.5 we are given two versions of the story that, after the murder of Hipparchus, Aristogiton was tortured and revealed the names of other plotters, one version being ascribed to 'democratic writers' and the other simply to 'others'. In 28.5, at the end of a list of democratic and aristocratic leaders, we read that Thucydides, Nicias and Theramenes, the last three of the aristocratic leaders, were the best of the more recent politicians; almost all agree about the first two, but opinion is divided over Theramenes: 'However, the judgement of those who are not superficial critics is that he did not destroy all regimes, as his detractors allege, but he supported all as long as they did nothing unlawful.' Probably those who are characterized as 'democratic writers' or 'superficial critics' are writers of polemical works, not of serious histories.

In about half the places where he mentions a disagreement, the author gives his own preference. In these cases he says not that he has evidence which proves that one version is correct (which is not to say that there was no such evidence), but that one seems more reasonable. In the story in chapter 6 that Solon gave advance information of his plans for the Shaking-off of Burdens to his friends, the hostile version is that he did it deliberately, and was himself one of the men who profited from this knowledge: but 'it is not plausible' that Solon would have behaved dishonourably in small things when he behaved honourably in great, so 'the accusation that he joined in the scheme must therefore be judged false'. In 7.4 some men think that the qualification for membership of Solon's second property class, the cavalry, was ability to maintain a horse, and they cite in support of their view the name of the class and equestrian dedications by members of it: 'Even so, it is more reasonable that the cavalry should have been defined by measures of produce like the five-hundred-bushel class.' (The author does not distinguish, as we should like, the questions how the class acquired its name and in what terms Solon defined the criteria for membership of it.) We are not told whether there was positive evidence that the criterion for membership of the cavalry and the lower classes was measures of produce, but we are not bound to conclude from the appeal to what is reasonable that there was no evidence. The same applies to what is said in 8.1–2 on the appointment of the archons: this time the author does not admit that there was a disagreement, but we can contrast his statement that the old practice was election by the Areopagus and the new was allotment from an elected short list from the highest property classes with the statement of Aristotle's *Politics* (II. 1273b–1274a, III. 1281b) that Solon left the practice of election by the people unchanged. To prove his case, he ought to have cited the relevant law of Solon; what he does is cite the law on the appointment of the treasurers of Athena, still in force in his own day as the law on the archons was not, which prescribed that they were to be appointed by lot from the highest class. Some scholars have thought that because he did not cite good evidence he cannot have had good evidence, and that the *Politics* is right and the *Athenian Constitution* is wrong; but I suspect that he did have the evidence, that Solon's laws survived and that he, or more probably his source, had consulted them, and that what he was doing here was not giving the basis of his conclusion but citing a familiar fact to confirm an unfamiliar one.

One form of argument which we do find is chronological. Chapter 17.2 states (in unusually strong language), 'It is ... palpable nonsense when people say that [Pisistratus] was loved by Solon ...: the chronology does not allow it, if you reckon up the life of each man and the archonship in which each died.' Our author had more facts than he chose to pass on to us, since we are given the year of Pisistratus's death (17.1) but not the year of Solon's death; in fact years of birth would have been more relevant, and in fact Solon was twenty to twenty-five years older than Pisistratus and chronologically there is nothing implausible about the story. When he tried to combine incompatible accounts, our author became badly confused. In 17.3–18.2 he deals with the sons of Pisistratus, and with the episode which led to the murder of Hipparchus. Chapter 18 begins by preparing us for the story as it had been told by Thucydides (VI.54), in which Hipparchus was the lover spurned by Harmodius, by describing Hipparchus as 'childish and amorous'; but then Hipparchus is jettisoned, and it is another son, Thessalus, 'bold and insolent', who is said to have loved Harmodius. If we combine the information in Herodotus (V.94) and Thucydides (VI.55), we conclude that Thessalus was Pisistratus's third son by his first wife, but in the *Athenian Constitution* Thessalus is said to be the additional name of a son by a later wife, so that he can be 'much younger' than Hippias and Hipparchus and more appropriate for the part of chief villain. Some scholars have thought that our author could not have been as careless as this, and that he gave the story as Thucydides had given it and the intrusion of Thessalus is to be blamed on a later interpolator; but I fear that the fault lies with our author himself.

The most obvious style for a historical work is sequential: first one thing happened, then a second and a third, then a fourth. However, one has only to look at Herodotus to realize that the sequential is not the only possible style: frequently he starts on one subject, then turns aside for a digression, and perhaps puts a sub-digression inside that, or a second digression after it, before he returns to his main subject; to help the reader to keep his bearings, he often uses very similar expressions at the beginning and end of a section or sub-section (a technique known as ring composition). There are traces of this in the *Athenian Constitution*, and the use of this technique sometimes explains why material is presented in what we should regard as an illogical order.

We have an example of ring composition in chapters 2–5:

a¹	After this there was strife for a long time between the notables and the masses (2.1).
b¹	For the Athenians' constitution was oligarchic in all other respects,
c¹	and in particular the poor were enslaved to the rich (2.2).
c²	The harshest and bitterest aspect of the constitution for the masses was the fact of their enslavement (2.3).
b²	The organization of the ancient constitution [before the time of Draco] was as follows.
d¹	Officials were appointed on the basis of good birth and wealth (3.1).
d²	The appointment of the archons was based on good birth and wealth (3.6).
b³	That is the outline of the first constitution.
e¹	Subsequently ... Draco enacted his ordinances (4.1).
[c³	As has been stated above, loans were on the security of the person, and the land was in the hands of a few (4.5).]
b⁴	While the state was organized in this way,
c⁴	and the many were enslaved to the few,
a²	the people rose against the notables. The strife was fierce, and they held out against one another for a long time (5.1–2).

2.1 introduces the theme of conflict; 2.2 gives two causes of conflict, the oligarchic constitution and the enslavement of the poor, and then proceeds to deal in detail with the second of those causes; 2.3 rounds off the enslavement of the poor, and at the same time with its mention of the constitution acts as a bridge to the first cause of conflict, the political; that is dealt with in chapter 3, and it is in order to open and close a ring that the basis for appointments is mentioned both at the beginning of the chapter and at the end. I believe that the 'Constitution of Draco' in chapter 4 is an addition to the original text of the *Athenian Constitution* (see pp. 32–3), but that the opening sentence of the chapter, mentioning Draco's enactment of his ordinances, belongs to the original text and not to the addition. It has been argued that we obtain a neater pattern without chapter 4, and that this confirms that the whole of the chapter is an addition; but ring composition is a flexible device, allowing any number of small rings within a larger one, and I think it likelier that the original text contained a section on the ordinances of Draco, most of which was deleted when the 'Constitution of Draco' was inserted. The reference to Draco in 3.1, and the restatement of the theme of chapter 2 in 4.5, both belong to the addition, and have been bracketed in the analysis given above. The beginning of chapter 5 rounds off the whole passage, mentioning first the political cause of conflict, then the social and economic, and finally the conflict itself.

Analysis of the chapters on Solon shows that these too were carefully planned. In 6.1 the clause 'and he enacted laws' interrupts what is otherwise a well-balanced sentence, and also interrupts the theme of economic reform: probably the explanation is that in 'Solon liberated the people ... by forbidding loans on the security of the person; and he enacted laws' the author is announcing the two themes of economic reform and legal (and political) reform, as he announced two themes in 2.1, and then he treats the economic reform in the remainder of chapter 6 and the legal and political reform in chapters 7–8. It seems strange to the modern reader that chapter 20, after devoting sections 1–3 to an account of Cleisthenes and Isagoras, should revert in sections 4–5 to the Alcmaeonids' responsibility for the overthrow of the tyranny; but this reference to the tyranny is the completion of a 'ring' which began with the reference to the tyranny in the first sentence of chapter 20.

As a stylist our author is uneven. There are passages where he has taken some care, trying to produce a balanced sentence. The last sentence of chapter 38 is the most striking instance:

a^1 Rhinon and his supporters
b^1 were praised for their good will towards the people:
c^1 having accepted responsibility under the oligarchy
c^2 they submitted to examination under the democracy,
b^2 and no complaint was made against them
d^1 either by those who had remained in the city
d^2 or by those who had returned from the Piraeus;
a^2 indeed, on account of this Rhinon was immediately elected general.

The first sentence of chapter 6 would be perfectly balanced, after its introductory phrase, but for the reference to Solon's enacting laws; and I have suggested above that the author inserted those words to announce in advance a theme to which he would return later. There are passages in the Greek where a pattern can be detected in the sequence of long and short syllables: this may have been deliberately intended, or it may simply be a by-product of the author's trying to write what he regarded as readable Greek. There are passages where he has tried to avoid monotony: 28.2–3 gives a long list of rival democratic and aristocratic leaders; a variety of different words are used to label the two sides, and the form of expression is varied also; in the case of Themistocles and Aristides the text is so abrupt that scholars have been able to argue about its meaning (I have added 'respectively' in the translation, to retain something of the flavour but make what I believe to be the meaning clear).

However, the effort to write good Greek is not sustained throughout. At the end of chapter 24, and in the summary of the first part, in 41.2, the text degenerates into an ungrammatical list. There are passages like that on Themistocles and Aristides in 28.2, where the meaning has not been made indisputably clear. Monotony is not always avoided: the first four sentences of chapter 7 contain four instances of the same Greek word for 'law', *nomos* (in three of the four instances the same form, the genitive plural *nomon*). In several places the text seems over-compressed, probably because the author is abbreviating from a longer original and has not taken enough trouble over his abbreviation: at the beginning of chapter 22, section 1 mentions among 'other new laws' of Cleisthenes the law on ostracism; that is left unexplained while section 2 is devoted to the councillors' oath and the appointment of generals; and then section 3 returns to the subject of ostracism. In vocabulary the author reflects his sources: passages derived from Herodotus use a great many Herodotean words, though occasionally not the words used in the corresponding passage of Herodotus. It has been suggested that the last sentence of chapter 38, analysed above, was copied from a work written at the beginning of the fourth century, when that kind of balanced writing was fashionable. Features of this kind are not surprising: they can be paralleled in the work of modern research students.

The second part of the *Athenian Constitution* gives an account of the working of the constitution in the author's own day. It may be analysed as follows; as before, the letters in the left-hand column refer to the sections into which I divide the translation.

In Aristotle's *Politics* the analysis of the elements of a constitution at the end of Book IV deals first with the citizen body, and then with 'the three parts of all constitutions': deliberation on public affairs, officials, and justice (1296b–1301a). The *Athenian Constitution* is similar but not identical in its analysis: there is no separate section on deliberation; all that is said on deliberation, and much of what is said on justice, is worked into the long section on officials. There is no catalogue of officials in Book IV of the *Politics*; there are catalogues at the end of Book VI (1321b–1323a), showing some resemblances to Athens but also some differences.

Another approach to our author's scheme can be found in the actual laws of Athens. The laws were revised at the end of the fifth century, and there is evidence that the revisers tried to produce a systematic code, in which laws on the same subject were grouped together. A fourth-century law which provided for an annual review of the code divided the laws into four categories: laws concerning the council; 'common' laws (probably laws common to all officials); laws for the nine archons; laws for the other officials (quoted by Demosthenes, *Against Timocrates* 20). If the 'common' laws are of a kind that need not be included in a study of the constitution, the other three categories are reflected fairly well in the arrangement of chapters 43–62; and it may be because the laws were organized in this way that our author has no separate section on deliberation, or on the assembly, but includes what he has to say on these matters in his treatment of the council.

In theory there are three kinds of source on which he could have drawn for his analysis of the constitution: the laws of Athens; observation of current practice; and earlier analyses of the constitution. In fact the last of these three can be ruled out, as we have no reason to believe that there were any earlier analyses, and in the main the account which we are given seems to be based on the actual laws. 56.7 deals with the archon's responsibility for orphans, heiresses and pregnant widows:

> He has the oversight of orphans, heiresses and women who at the death of their husband claim to be pregnant; and he has full power to impose a summary fine on the offenders or to bring them before the jury-court.

The law corresponding to that sentence is quoted in a speech preserved with those of Demosthenes (*Against Macartatus* 75):

> Let the archon be responsible for orphans, heiresses, deserted houses, and women who remain in the houses of their deceased husbands and assert that they are pregnant. Let him be responsible for these, and not allow any one to commit outrage with respect to them. If any one commits outrage or does anything illegal, let him have full power to impose a summary fine within his competence; if he thinks that the offender deserves a greater penalty, let him give a summons at five days' notice, writing at the end the assessment that he thinks appropriate, and bring the accused before the *heliaea*; if he obtains a conviction, let the *heliaea* assess for the convicted man what he should suffer or pay.

Our author abbreviates; where the law orders what is to happen, he states what does happen; to a considerable extent he uses the language of the law, but he substitutes current for archaic language in using 'claim' (*skeptesthai*) for 'assert' (*phaskein*), and 'jury-court' (*dikasterion*) for *heliaea* (the name of Solon's appeal court, out of which the jury-courts had developed). It should nevertheless be clear that our author's sentence is derived from the law. What is said about the different homicide courts in 57.3–4 bears the same relationship to quotations from the law which we find in Demosthenes' speech *Against Aristocrates*. Although the whole of our author's account is a series of statements, not orders, he frequently inserts the words 'the laws prescribe' or 'the law prescribes'. The existence of a revised and organized code of laws will have made this piece of research easy.

Since the *Athenian Constitution* was written by a member of Aristotle's school in Athens (possibly but not necessarily an Athenian citizen), it is hard to believe that it owes nothing to observation of current practice. There are several notes on differences between earlier practice and current practice, which may be derived from the original law and an amending law, or may be derived from the author's own general knowledge; the anecdote in 45.1 (the only anecdote in the second part) cannot have been found in the laws, nor can the two references in 60.2 and 61.2 to powers which legally exist but are not now exercised. Occasionally, the author uses language which cannot be based on the laws: in 43.6, 'Sometimes business is taken without a preliminary vote' (presumably an impatient summary of a law which listed occasions when this could happen); in 64.2, 'The man whose ticket is drawn is called the inserter.'

For an analysis of the constitution the natural arrangement is a division into sections and sub-sections, and this is what the author has provided. Sometimes, in accordance with the principles of ring composition, a section is ended with a phrase echoing the phrase which began it. The section on the nine archons uses the following introductory and resumptive phrases:

a¹   As for the so-called nine archons ... (55.1)
b¹   The archon ... (56.2)
b²   Those are the responsibilities of the archon.
c¹   The *basileus* ... (57.1)
d¹   The polemarch ... (58.1)
d²   ... the polemarch does for metics (58.3).
e¹   The *thesmothetae* ... (59.1)
a²   The allotment of jurors is carried out by all the nine archons ... (59.7)
a³   That is the position with regard to the nine archons (60.1).

In the section on the council we find:

n¹   There is a council of five hundred appointed by lot (43.2).
o¹   In general the council cooperates in the administrative work of the officials (47.1).
o²   In general, one might say, the council cooperates in the administrative work of the other officials (49.5).
n²   That is the work handled by the council (50.1).

However, the author's use of this technique was less than perfect. The sentence which ends chapter 49 would be more appropriately placed at the end of chapter 48. Within the section on the nine archons, the sub-section on the archon is given a formal ending, and the sub-section on the polemarch has an informal ending (in a sentence which is not obviously a conclusion but which does use the polemarch's title again), but there is no ending to the sub-sections on the *basileus* and the *thesmothetae*. There is no ending to the major section on officials which runs from chapter 43 to chapter 62; and at the end of chapter 69 there is nothing to indicate that this is the end of the section on the jury-courts and also of the whole work (there is no reason to suppose that it is not the end of the whole work but that a concluding section has been lost).

As in the first part, there are attempts to avoid monotony – we are not told in exactly the same words each time that there were ten so-and-sos, one appointed by lot from each tribe – but the author could have done more to vary his expression if he had thought it important to do so. As in the first part, there are places where the text is too compressed: the abrupt remark in 43.6, 'Sometimes business is taken without a preliminary vote', is the only mention of the 'preliminary vote' in the text, and as it happens there are few other references to it in other surviving texts and we remain uncertain when and how it was used. On the whole the arrangement of the material is methodical, but there appear to be some lapses: the election of military officers, in 44.4, would be better placed with the other regular business of the assembly, in chapter 43; the road-builders, in 54.1, would be better placed in chapters 50–51 with the other officials responsible for city facilities. The final chapters, on the mechanics of the jury-courts, proved too difficult for the author: if a complicated process is to be made intelligible to a reader who is unfamiliar with it, the material must be arranged in such a way that each new item can be understood on the basis of the items presented before it, but this has not always been achieved. In chapter 63 equipment for the allotment of jurors, including boxes to receive the jurors' tickets, is mentioned before the qualification for jury service and the fact that each man who has been registered for service has a ticket; the size of juries in public suits is not mentioned until 68.1, and the size of juries in private suits, having been given in 53.3, is not mentioned at all in this section. In some cases material which the reader needs is not supplied at all: the purpose of the 'official token' mentioned in 65.2 is not explained; it seems most likely that the time allowances of 67.2 were for private suits only, and that the 'measured-out day' of 67.3–5 was used not merely for some but for all public suits, but the author does not say so.

There are some surprising omissions: 54.3–5 lists three public secretaries; in contemporary documents there is evidence for six, including a secretary 'in charge of decrees' who ought to be parallel to the one 'in charge of laws' in section 4, and there is no obvious reason why the author should have picked on the three whom he does mention. There are matters on which omission has been suspected but scholars have been unable to agree. 42.1 does not say that men had to be born in wedlock to be Athenian citizens, but it can plausibly be argued that this was required; 42.2 and 53.4–5 imply that all citizens had to perform two years' cadet service after they came of age and to serve as arbitrators in the year in which they reached the age of sixty, but the cadets' training was hoplite training, and it can be argued that the members of the lowest property class, who were not required to fight as hoplites, were not required to serve as cadets or as arbitrators: in each of these cases I am among those who suspect that the author has not told the whole truth. However, though he is guilty of omissions, we have no reason to think that any of the facts which he does report is wrong. He has kept fairly strictly to his task of describing the constitution. Argument is rarer than in the first part (but there is an instance in 54.3); there is no comment on the merits and defects of the constitution, and no comparison between the Athenian constitution and other constitutions.

The constitution which is described here was overthrown in 321; and Athenian control of the island of Samos, mentioned in the present tense in 62.2, came to an end in 322. Chapter 42 describes, without any sign that it is a novelty, a programme of compulsory cadet training instituted about 335/4, and some of the regular postings for generals mentioned in 61.1 seem still not to have existed as late as 333/2. The *Athenian Constitution* should therefore have been written, or at any rate completed, between 332 and 322.

There are signs that the text as we have it incorporates some late insertions, and that an earlier edition which did not contain those insertions was current in the ancient world. 54.7 ends with an addition to the list of quadrennial festivals, dated 329/8 and qualified by 'now' (it is the only date given in the second part); it reads very much as an afterthought; it is possible, though by no means certain, that the lexicographer Pollux (of the second century AD) used a text which did not contain this afterthought. 51.3 mentions an increase in the number of corn-guardians, which seems to have taken place in the 320s; in this case there is nothing awkward about the actual text, and the text as we have it was used by Photius (of the ninth century AD), but it is likely that Harpocration (possibly of the second century AD) used a text which mentioned only the earlier number of corn-guardians. Another awkward passage is 46.1, which begins with triremes, then mentions 'triremes or quadriremes ... whichever the people decide', but ends simply with triremes again: Athens' navy included some quadriremes by 330/29, and quinqueremes, not mentioned in our text, first appear in 325/4; there are no later texts derived from this passage, which might help us, but it does seem likely that the passage was originally written to refer to triremes only, revised to allow for quadriremes, but not revised again to allow for quinqueremes.

Two additions can be detected in the historical part of the work. The first is the 'Constitution of Draco' in chapter 4: what arouses suspicion is not the disagreement between the *Athenian Constitution* and Aristotle's *Politics* (II.1274b), which shows only that the constitution was unknown to Aristotle when he referred to Draco in the *Politics*, but the fact that, although the *Athenian Constitution* circulated widely in antiquity, no other surviving text refers to the 'Constitution of Draco'. The story of Themistocles and Ephialtes in 25.3–4 appears otherwise only in an ancient introduction to Isocrates' *Areopagitic*, though Plutarch frequently cites the *Athenian*

Constitution, and we should expect him to mention the story in his life of *Themistocles*, if only to reject it. The natural conclusion is that the version of the *Athenian Constitution* which was most commonly used in the ancient world did not contain these passages. The theory of late insertions is reinforced when we notice that the story of Themistocles is joined very awkwardly to the murder of Ephialtes, at the end of 25.4; and that, when the 'Constitution of Draco' was added, references to it seem to have been added in 3.1 and 41.2, and the reference in 41.2 disastrously interrupts a numbered list of changes in the constitution. Unfortunately, in each of these cases the material added appears to be false: the 'Constitution of Draco' is unacceptable as a constitution earlier than that of Solon, and seems to have been invented in the late fifth or the fourth century; Themistocles was ostracized and left Athens several years before Ephialtes attacked the Areopagus.

What we have, then, is a text written at the end of the 330s, and revised to take account of some innovations of the 320s and of two unfortunate discoveries of new historical material. The first edition may have been put into circulation by its author. The revision may or may not have been done by the original author, but almost certainly it was done in the Aristotelian school in the 320s: later there would have been no point in bringing up to date the description of a constitution that had been overthrown, and the references to Draco in 3.1 and 41.2 suggest deliberate revision rather than an individual reader's annotation in his own copy. Probably, if Aristotle had not left Athens, and the democracy had not been overthrown, the process of keeping the work up to date would have continued. For Aristotle's school, the task of collecting evidence was never at an end: the student may have deposited a copy of his dissertation and have left the school, but the file was not closed.

The *Athenian Constitution* is not a masterpiece; its author was an average student. The historical part, however, contains a great deal of material that has not been preserved for us in any other text: much of it is very important to the historian either because it provides him with facts which he would not otherwise know or because it gives him a different slant on facts which are available elsewhere, but some of it is of poor quality and is important only as evidence of what a fourth-century writer could believe. What the author has done is somewhat different from what any earlier historian had done, in that he has compiled not a general history or even a history of Athens but more specifically a history of the Athenian constitution. The second part is more strikingly original: as far as we know, a factual account of how the constitution of a Greek city state worked had never been attempted by anyone until Aristotle's school started collecting constitutions; and our author, who for his history read many books but did not engage in original research, based his analysis on the actual laws which governed the working of the constitution. We do not know who he was; we cannot compare his work with the other 157 constitutions; but he has left us a book of great interest and importance.

My main aim in translating the *Athenian Constitution* has been to convey the author's meaning clearly: to help the reader I have split long sentences into shorter ones, have changed the constructions, and have added words that are not in the Greek text to make explicit what it leaves implicit. However, as far as considerations of acceptable English would allow, I have tried to reproduce something of the flavour of the original; so the translation follows the original in being sometimes varied and sometimes repetitive in its vocabulary, and in occasionally moving awkwardly from one topic to another or degenerating from grammatical prose into an ungrammatical list. Except in cases where a translation would be meaningless, I have translated technical terms rather than giving versions of the Greek words: both Greek and translated versions of all technical terms will be found in the Glossary. In translating and in explaining the text I have normally given simply the view which I believe to be right, without drawing attention to alternative views (supporting arguments, and references to alternative views, may be found in my large *Commentary on the Aristotelian Athenaion Politeia*; but in the notes on 21.4 and 44.1 I mention one point on which a book published since my *Commentary* has led me to change my mind, and an inscription published in *Hesperia* 52 (1983), pp. 48–63, has affected what I say in the notes on 3.5 and 15.4 on the location of buildings). To help readers who use this translation together with a Greek text, I do draw attention in the Notes to points where I disagree with other editors as to what the correct Greek text should be. For the *Epitome of Heraclides* I have given a literal translation of the Greek text of M. R. Dilts (see Bibliography): the Greek text is included in most editions of the *Athenian Constitution*, but their editors have been too willing to correct the compiler's glaring errors. Much of my translation was written without reference to any other, but at difficult points I have consulted several translations, and I have occasionally borrowed an expression on which I could not improve.

I should like to thank the Oxford University Press for permission to re-use here material from my *Commentary*; and to the acknowledgements in the Preface to my *Commentary* I should like to add my thanks to the administrators of the Fulbright-Hays travel grants (accidentally omitted there), Mrs M. Adamson, Professor T. J. Saunders, the Editor of the Penguin Classics Mrs Radice, and all who have contributed to the production of this book.

THE ATHENIAN CONSTITUTION

The beginning of the work, equivalent to about four pages in this translation, has not survived (see p. 13). It seems to have dealt briefly with the following topics. Cecrops, born from the soil, was the first king of Athens; Cranaus, likewise born from the soil, succeeded him and founded a dynasty. In the reign of Erechtheus Athens was attacked by Eleusis and the Thracians; the office of polemarch was created for Ion, son of the Peloponnesian king Xuthus and Erechtheus' daughter Creüsa, and he led the Athenians to victory. He then settled in Athens; and the Athenians were divided into four tribes named after his four sons, each with its tribal head, and into two classes of Farmers and Workers for the People. King Pandion added Megara to the kingdom, and divided the enlarged kingdom between his four sons: Aegeus took the city of Athens and the surrounding plain, Pallas the coast, Lycus the northern hills, and Nisus Megara. However, Lycus was driven out by Aegeus and fled to Asia Minor; Nisus was killed and Megara captured by Minos of Crete; and, when Theseus was acknowledged as Aegeus' heir, Pallas attacked and Theseus defeated him. Theseus made a proclamation, calling on the inhabitants of the twelve cities of Attica to make Athens their one political centre. He distinguished an aristocracy of the Well-born from the rest of the citizen body, and perhaps created the council of the Areopagus; and in some way he reduced the power of the monarchy. Theseus and Pirithous captured Helen from Sparta, but then were themselves captured when they tried to carry off Persephone from the underworld. In Theseus' absence Menestheus, a great-grandson of Erechtheus, roused the nobles and people against him and with the help of Helen's brothers was made king in his place. Theseus, released by Heracles but unable to regain control of Athens, sailed to Scyros, where he was lured to his death by king Lycomedes; his remains were brought back to Athens by Cimon after the Persian Wars (c. 476).

Menestheus either died in the Trojan War or was expelled after it, and Theseus' son Demophon recovered the throne of Athens. Later, in the reign of the elderly Thymoetes, Melanthus, a fugitive from Pylos, accepted a challenge from Xanthus of Boeotia on condition that he should become king if he won; thus a new dynasty was founded. Melanthus was succeeded by his son Codrus; but Codrus's sons were soft and given to luxury, and so Medon was induced to accept the new office of archon for life in place of the kingship. The new office continued to be held by descendants of Codrus; after some time, tenure was reduced from life to ten years. Hippomenes, the fourth of the ten-year archons, chafed under his family's loss of power and wanted to recover the old power of the kings; but after he had caught his daughter Limone in adultery and to kill her had shut her up with a horse in an empty house, he was deprived of his office, and the archonship was thrown open to all the Well-born. After three more ten-year archons the term of office was again reduced, to one year, the first annual archon being Creon (683/2). From this point our author may have passed directly to the attempt of Cylon to make himself tyrant (chapter 1, below).

This was the legendary history of Athens as it had been systematized by the fourth century BC. Of the actual history little can be said. The Mycenaean kingdoms collapsed in the twelfth century; in the dark age which followed, Athens remained inhabited, and was one of the first cities to show signs of recovery; it is likely that some of those who migrated from the Greek mainland to the Aegean islands and Asia Minor had links with or passed through Athens. By the seventh century the whole of Attica, about 1,000 square miles, formed a single state ruled from Athens; Eleusis, in the west of Attica, was incorporated later than the remainder. There was a ruling caste known as the Well-born, the families which had emerged most successful from the dark age; there was a wider circle of clans, which had organized their dependants around them in brotherhoods; but the division into Farmers and Workers for the People makes only one dubious appearance in the historical period (13.2), and is probably a product of later theorizing. Also the people were divided into four tribes, each subdivided into three thirds. The principal officers of state were the nine archons, appointed annually from the ranks of the Well-born; three had individual titles and were senior to the other six (see chapter 3), and the fact that one of these was called basileus, *'king', suggests that earlier there had been a hereditary king; it may be true that the one styled archon had been appointed annually since 683/2. The council of the Areopagus had come to consist of former holders of the nine archonships.*

B CYLON (Chapter 1)

Cylon, who had been a victor in the Olympic games in 640 and was married to the daughter of Theagenes tyrant of Megara, collected supporters including a force from Megara and attempted to seize the Acropolis; the attempt failed, and they were besieged on the Acropolis; when they took refuge at the altar as suppliants (see 43.6) they were promised that their lives would be spared, but the promise was broken; the archon, Megacles of the Alcmaeonid family, was held to blame for this. There followed strife between the supporters of Cylon and the supporters of Megacles, and war broke out between Athens and Megara. Eventually the Alcmaeonids were made to stand trial and were condemned: the family was placed under a curse, and both the living and the bones of the dead were expelled from Attica; Athens was ritually purified by Epimenides of Crete.

Tyranny and the killing of suppliants were both offences in the eyes of later Athenians, and differing, partisan accounts of the affair could be presented. Herodotus (V.71) and Thucydides (I.126) both tell the story, but neither of them names Megacles, or the men who appear in the first surviving sentences of the Athenian Constitution, *Myron and Epimenides. The account in Plutarch's Solon (12) is consistent with what survives here, and the two are probably derived from the same source.*

1

... the prosecutor being Myron, and the jurors men qualified by good birth and swearing an oath over sacred victims. When the curse was pronounced, the remains of the original offenders were uprooted from their graves and expelled, and their descendants were sent into perpetual exile. It was on these terms that Epimenides the Cretan purified the city.

C BETWEEN CYLON AND SOLON (Chapters 2–4)

Chapters 2–12 form an organized whole, 2–4 being devoted to the causes of the economic and political discontent in Athens at the beginning of the sixth century, and 5–12 to Solon's attempt to deal with this discontent. There are a few allusions to Solon by Herodotus, who treats him as a sage, a lawgiver and a poet rather than as an economic and constitutional reformer; he is not mentioned by Thucydides. Probably the main source of these chapters was either a history of Athens (an Atthis) or a separate work on Solon; there is substantial agreement with Plutarch's Solon, which uses material from the Athenian Constitution *or its source or both. On Solon's reforms there was good information available to later writers, in Solon's poems and very probably in his actual laws (see 7.1 with note); but on the state of Athens before his reforms it is unlikely that much direct evidence survived, though on some matters inferences could be drawn from his laws. We may accept that many peasants were dependent on an overlord, cultivating their land on condition that they surrendered a proportion of the produce to him, and that they and others were liable to be enslaved if they fell inextricably into debt; and that political power was exercised by the Well-born, who were for the most part the richest citizens, through the nine archonships and the council of the Areopagus.*

Two passages interrupt the plan of these chapters: the account of a 'Constitution of Draco' in chapter 4, and that of Solon's reform of measures, weights and coinage, in chapter 10 (on which see pp. 45–6). Athens' first written code of laws was generally attributed to Draco. The 'Constitution of Draco', however, contains details which cannot be authentic but point to invention in the late fifth or the fourth century; there is no other allusion to such a constitution elsewhere in ancient literature, and Aristotle's Politics *(II. 1274b) states that Draco enacted laws for the existing constitution; in 41.2 the numbered list of changes in the constitution has been clumsily altered to include a reference to Draco. Probably the original version of the* Athenian Constitution, *which circulated most widely in antiquity, contained not this constitution, but the first two sentences of chapter 4 as we have it, followed by an account of Draco's code of laws; subsequently the author or another member of Aristotle's school discovered the constitution and was deceived by it, substituted it for the original material in chapter 4, and in the hope of making the revision less obvious inserted the references to Draco which we have in 3.1 and 41.2.*

2

(1) After this there was strife for a long time between the notables and the masses. (2) For the Athenians' constitution was oligarchic in all other respects, and in particular the poor were enslaved to the rich – themselves and their children and their wives. The poor were called dependants and sixth-parters, since it was for the rent of a sixth that they worked the fields of the rich. All the land was in the hands of a few, and if the poor failed to pay their rents both they and their children were liable to seizure. All loans were made on the security of the person until the time of Solon: he was the first champion of the people. (3) The harshest and bitterest aspect of the constitution for the masses was the fact of their enslavement, though they were discontented on other grounds too: it could be said that there was nothing in which they had a share.

3

(1) The organization of the ancient constitution before the time of Draco was as follows. Officials were appointed on the basis of good birth and wealth; at first men held office for life, subsequently for ten years. (2) The first and most important of the officials were the *basileus*, the polemarch and the archon. The oldest office was that of the *basileus*, the traditional ruler. Secondly the office of polemarch was added, because some of the *basileis* were not strong warriors: this is why the Athenians sent for Ion when they were in need. (3) The last to be created was the office of archon. Most place this in the time of Medon, but some place it in the time of Acastus: champions of the latter view cite in support the fact that the nine archons swear that they will abide by their oaths as in the time of Acastus, and claim that it was in his time that the descendants of Codrus stepped down from the kingship in exchange for the rights given to the archon. Whichever view is right, it would make little difference to the chronology. That the office of archon was the last of these is confirmed by the fact that the archon is not responsible for any of the traditional festivals, as the *basileus* and polemarch are, but only for the newer creations. This is how it has more recently become the principal office of state, being augmented by newly

created functions. (4) The *thesmothetae* were instituted many years later, when the term of office had already become a single year, to write down the statutes and preserve them for the resolution of disputes: for that reason this alone of the chief offices has never been held for longer than a year. (5) That is the chronological sequence of the offices. The nine archons used not all work together: the *basileus* occupied what is now called the Bucoleum, near the town hall (as an indication of this, the ritual encounter and marriage of the *basileus*' wife and Dionysus takes place there), the archon the town hall, and the polemarch the Epilyceum (which used to be called the *polemarcheum*, but was named Epilyceum when the polemarch Epilycus rebuilt and restored it); the *thesmothetae* occupied the *thesmotheteum*. In the time of Solon they all came together in the *thesmotheteum*. They had full power to give a final judgement in lawsuits, not simply to hold a preliminary inquiry as they do now. (6) The council of the Areopagus had the function of watching over the laws, and it administered most and the greatest of the city's affairs, having full power to chastise and punish all the disorderly. The appointment of the archons was based on good birth and wealth, and it was the archons who became members of the Areopagus: for that reason membership of the Areopagus alone has remained to this day an office held for life.

4

(1) That is the outline of the first constitution. Subsequently, a short time afterwards, in the archonship of Aristaechmus [621/0], Draco enacted his ordinances. His organization was of the following kind. (2) Political rights had been given to those who bore arms. The nine archons and the treasurers were elected from men with an unencumbered estate of not less than ten minas, and the other, lesser, officials from the men who bore arms; the generals and the cavalry commanders from those who declared an unencumbered estate of not less than one hundred minas, and who had legitimate sons, born in wedlock, over ten years old. These officials were required to take security from the *prytanes*, generals and cavalry commanders of the previous year until they had undergone their examination, enlisting, as guarantors of each, four men from the same property class as

the generals and cavalry commanders. (3) There was a council of four hundred and one, appointed by lot from the men possessing political rights. Lots were to be drawn for this and for the other offices among the men over thirty years old, and the same man was not to hold office a second time until all had held office once; then the allotment was to be repeated from the beginning. If a member of the council was absent from a meeting when the council or assembly was sitting, he would be fined three drachmae if he was a member of the five-hundred-bushel class, two drachmae if a cavalryman, one drachma if a ranker. (4) The council of the Areopagus was guardian of the laws, and watched over the officials to see that they exercised their office in accordance with the laws. A man who was wronged could make a denunciation to the council of the Areopagus, indicating the law under which he was wronged. (5) As has been stated above, loans were on the security of the person, and the land was in the hands of a few.

D SOLON (Chapters 5–12)

Chapters 5–12 are probably derived for the most part either from an Atthis *or from a separate work on Solon, the same source as was used for chapters 2–4; Plutarch's* Solon *made use of this source or the* Athenian Constitution *or both. Since there was good evidence for what Solon had done, in his poems and his laws, our author was able to treat Solon at some length.*

The Athenians, in a state of tension between rich and poor, chose Solon to be archon and mediator (chapter 5). He liberated the people by cancelling debts and banning loans on the security of the person (6), produced a new code of laws in place of Draco's (7.1–2), divided the citizens into four classes according to the produce of their land, and assigned different degrees of political power to the different classes (7.3–8.5); three of his measures are singled out as particularly democratic (9). He also reformed Athens' measures, weights and coinage (10). Finding that he had pleased neither side, he left Athens for ten years, during which his laws were not to be altered (11). The section on Solon ends with quotations from his poems, to illustrate his political intentions (12). After the summing-up of Solon's reforms in chapter 9, the addition of further reforms in chapter 10 interrupts what is otherwise a well organized section. Plutarch (Solon 15) quotes from the Atthis *of Androtion a different account of the reform of measures, weights and coinage, and our author has perhaps gone out of his way to insert what he believed to be the truth on a matter where Androtion was mistaken.*

It appears that Solon was concerned essentially with two problems: agrarian discontent, arising from the servitude of the sixth-parters and the risk which they and other peasants ran of falling hopelessly into debt and being enslaved; and political discontent, due partly to distrust of the aristocratic officials, even after the laws had been published by Draco, and partly to ambition for political equality among men who were outside the circle of the Well-born but were no less rich than them. Though Solon was accepted by all as a mediator, and is said in chapter 5 to have been 'of the middle sort', the quotations in that chapter show that he had attracted attention by championing the poor and unprivileged against the rich and powerful; but he refused to make himself tyrant, and was genuinely moderate in his settlement, which therefore annoyed the rich without satisfying the poor. Discontent persisted, to be exploited by Pisistratus in the next generation (see chapters 13–19).

5

(1) While the state was organized in this way, and the many were enslaved to the few, the people rose against the notables. (2) The strife was fierce, and they held out against one another for a long time. Eventually the two sides agreed to appoint Solon as reconciler and archon [594/3], and entrusted the state to him. He had written the elegy which begins:

> I know, and anguish of heart lies within me,
> When I look on the eldest land of Ionia
> Being slain.

In this poem he fights and disputes against each side on behalf of the other, and afterwards he urges them to join together in putting an end to the contention dwelling in them. (3) Solon was by birth and repute one of the leading citizens, but by wealth and position one of the middle sort. The other evidence agrees on this, and in particular he bears witness to it himself in these poems, in which he urges the rich not to be grasping:

But quieten the strong spirit in your hearts,
  You who have pushed through to glut yourselves with many good things,
  And in moderation lay aside your ambitious thoughts.
We shall not allow you to proceed like this,
  Nor will these things be wholesome for you.

Altogether he everywhere lays the blame for the strife on the rich: for that reason at the beginning of the poem he expresses his fear of their 'love of money and arrogance', suggesting that this was the cause of the ill-feeling.

6

(1) On gaining control of affairs Solon liberated the people, both immediately and for the future, by forbidding loans on the security of the person; and he enacted laws; and he made a cancellation of debts, both private and public, which the Athenians call the Shaking-off of Burdens, since by means of it they shook off the weight lying on them. (2) Some people try to slander Solon in this matter. When Solon was about to bring in the Shaking-off of Burdens, he mentioned it in advance to some of the notables; then, according to the democrats, he was outmanoeuvred by his friends, or, according to hostile sources, he joined in the scheme himself. The men he had spoken to raised loans and bought up large tracts of land, and not long afterwards the cancellation of debts took place and made them rich. This is said to be how men who were later reputed to be of ancient wealth had come by their riches. (3) However, the democratic version of the story is more credible. Solon was so moderate and impartial in other respects that, when he could have got the rest of the people into his power and made himself tyrant over the city, he instead accepted the hatred of both sides and set a higher value on honour and the safety of the city than on his own advantage; so it is not plausible that he should have defiled himself in so petty and easily detected a matter. (4) That he had the opportunity to become tyrant is evident from the diseased

state of affairs: he frequently mentions it in his poetry, and everyone else agrees. The accusation that he joined in the scheme must therefore be judged false.

7

(1) Solon established a constitution and enacted other laws, and the Athenians ceased to use the ordinances of Draco apart from those concerning homicide. The laws were inscribed on the *kyrbeis* and set up in the Portico of the Basileus, and everyone swore to observe them. The nine archons, when swearing their oath at the stone, solemnly undertook to dedicate a golden statue if they should transgress any of the laws, and so even today they continue to swear this. (2) Solon secured the laws against alteration for a hundred years, and he organized the constitution as follows. (3) He divided the citizens into four classes by an assessment of wealth, as they had been divided before: the five-hundred-bushel class, the cavalry, the rankers and the labourers. He distributed among the five-hundred-bushel class, the cavalry and the rankers the major offices, such as the nine archons, the treasurers, the sellers, the Eleven and the *colacretae*, assigning offices to the members of each class according to the level of their assessment. To those registered in the labourers' class he gave only membership of the assembly and jury-courts. (4) A man was registered in the five-hundred-bushel class if the produce of his own estate amounted to five hundred measures of dry and liquid goods taken together; in the cavalry class if it amounted to three hundred. (Some people say that the cavalry were defined as those capable of maintaining a horse. They cite both the name of the class, as a reflection of that criterion, and also ancient dedications; for there stands on the Acropolis a statue of Diphilus bearing this inscription:

> Anthemion son of Diphilus made this dedication to the gods,
> Having exchanged the labourers' for the cavalry class.

There is a horse standing beside him, as an indication that this is what the cavalry class signifies. Even so, it is more reasonable that the cavalry should have been defined by measures of produce like the five-hundred-bushel class.) The rankers' class comprised those whose produce amounted to two hundred measures in both kinds; the remainder belonged to the labourers' class, and had no share in office-holding. For this reason, even today, when a candidate for allotment to any office is asked which class he belongs to, no one will reply that he belongs to the labourers' class.

8

(1) Solon had the officials appointed by allotment from a short list of men elected by each of the tribes. For the nine archons each tribe elected ten candidates, and lots were drawn among these: because of this it is still the practice for each of the tribes to pick ten men by lot, and then for an allotment to be made among them. That Solon stipulated appointment by lot from the property-classes is confirmed by the law on the treasurers, which remains in use even today: it orders the appointment of the treasurers by lot from the five-hundred-bushel class. (2) That is the law which Solon enacted concerning the nine archons. Originally the council of the Areopagus on its own called men up, judged them and made its disposition, appointing the most suitable man to each of the offices for the year. (3) In Solon's constitution there were four tribes, as before, and four tribal heads. Each of the tribes was divided into three thirds and into twelve *naucrariae*. There were officials called *naucrari* in charge of the *naucrariae*, with responsibility for income and expenditure: for that reason in the laws of Solon which are no longer in use we often find written 'the *naucrari* shall exact' and 'disburse from the naucraric silver'. (4) Solon instituted a council of four hundred, one hundred from each tribe, and appointed the council of the Areopagus to guard the laws, just as previously it had been overseer of the constitution. In general it watched over most and the greatest of the city's affairs; it corrected wrongdoers, having full power to punish and chastise, and depositing its penalties on the Acropolis without recording the reason for the penalty; and in particular it tried those charged with conspiring to dissolve the democracy, under the law of denunciation which Solon enacted to deal with them. (5) Seeing that the city was often in a state of strife, and that some of the citizens through apathy accepted whatever might happen, he enacted a special law to deal with them, that if when the city was

torn by strife anyone should refuse to place his arms at the disposal
of either side he should be outlawed and have no share in the city.

9

(1) That is how the officials were dealt with. The following seem
to be the three most democratic features of Solon's constitution:
first and most important, the ban on loans on the security of the
person; next, permission for anyone who wished to seek retribution
for those who were wronged; and third, the one which is said
particularly to have contributed to the power of the masses, the
right of appeal to the jury-court – for when the people are masters
of the vote they are masters of the state. (2) In addition, because
his laws were not written simply and clearly, but were like the law
on inheritance and heiresses, it was inevitable that many disputes
should arise and that the jury-court should decide all things both
public and private. Some people think that he made his laws unclear
deliberately, in order that the power of decision should rest with
the people. However, it is not likely that he was unclear for that
reason, but rather because it is impossible to define what is best
in general terms. It is not right to estimate his intentions from present-
day practice: one should judge from the rest of his political
programme.

10

(1) Those appear to be the democratic features in Solon's laws. Before
his legislation he carried out his cancellation of debts, and after that
his increase in the measures and weights, and in the currency.
(2) Under Solon the measures were made larger than those of
Pheidon, and the mina, which previously weighed seventy drachmae,
was raised to the full 100. The old standard coin was a two-drachma
piece. He also fixed weights with regard to the coinage, at the rate
of sixty-three minas' worth of coins to the talent weight, and the
extra three minas were assigned in proportion to the stater and the
other weights.

11

(1) Solon organized the constitution in the manner stated. Since men persisted in coming up to him and complaining about his laws, criticizing some and questioning others, and he did not want either to change them or to stay in Athens and incur hostility, he went on his travels, going to Egypt to trade and to see the sights, and saying that he would not return for ten years: he did not think it right that he should stay and expound his laws, but everyone should simply do what he had written. (2) Moreover, it turned out that many of the notables had become disenchanted with him because of the cancellation of debts, and that both parties regretted his appointment because his settlement was contrary to their expectations. The people had thought that he would carry out a complete redistribution of property, while the notables had thought that he would restore them to the same position as before, or make only small changes. But Solon was opposed to both; and, while he could have combined with whichever party he chose and become tyrant, he preferred to incur the hatred of both by saving his country and legislating for the best.

12

(1) Everyone agrees that that is how he acted, and he has mentioned it himself in his poetry, as follows:

> I gave to the people as much esteem as is sufficient for them,
> Not detracting from their honour or reaching out to take it;
> And to those who had power and were admired for their wealth
> I declared that they should have nothing unseemly.
> I stood holding my mighty shield against both,
> And did not allow either to win an unjust victory.

(2) Here is another passage in which he shows how the masses should be treated:

> This is how the people will best follow their leaders:
> If they are neither unleashed nor restrained too much.
> For excess breeds insolence, when great prosperity comes
> To men who are not sound of mind.

(3) Again, in another passage he speaks of those who wanted a redistribution of land:

> They came for plunder, full of rich hopes,
> Each of them expecting to find great prosperity,
> And expecting me to reveal an iron will behind my velvet speech.
> Their talk then was vain; but now they are angry with me,
> And all look askance at me as if I were their enemy.
> It should not be. What I said, I have done with the help of the gods:
> I did nothing in vain, nor was it my pleasure
> To act through the violence of tyranny, or that the bad
> Should have equal shares with the good in our country's rich land.

(4) Again, on the cancellation of debts, and on those who were previously slaves and were freed by the Shaking-off of Burdens, he says:

> Of the things for which I summoned the people to assemble,
> Did I finish before I had achieved all?
> I might call to witness in the justice which time brings
> The greatest and best mother of the Olympian deities,
> Black Earth, from which I removed
> The markers that were fixed in many places,
> The Earth which once was enslaved but now is free.
> To Athens, to their home of divine origin,
> I brought back many who had been sold,
> Some unjustly, some justly,
> And some who had fled out of dire necessity,
> Who no longer spoke the Athenian tongue
> After wandering in many places.
> Others, who were subjected here to shameful slavery,
> Fearing the whims of their masters, I set free.
> These things I achieved by my power,
> Harnessing together force and justice;
> And I persevered in my promises.
> I wrote down ordinances for bad and good alike,
> Providing straight justice for each man.
> If another man had taken up the goad as I did,
> A man of malicious counsel and greed,
> He would not have restrained the people. If I had been willing
> To do what the people's opponents then desired,
> Or again to do what the other party threatened to them,

This city would have been bereft of many men.
For that reason, setting up a defence on all sides,
I turned about like a wolf among many dogs.

(5) Again, he reproaches both parties for the complaints which they afterwards levelled against him:

If I am to reproach the people openly, I say
That what they now have their eyes would not have seen
Even in their dreams.
And those who are greater and more fortunate in life
Should praise me and make me their friend.

If some other man, he says, had obtained this position,

He would not have restrained the people, nor have stopped
Until he had stirred up the milk and taken away its cream.
But I stood in the middle ground between them
Like a marker.

E BETWEEN SOLON AND PISISTRATUS (Chapter 13)

Solon's settlement failed to satisfy either side, and discontent persisted. In 13.1–2, presumably derived from the published list of archons through an Atthis, we read of two occasions when no archon was appointed and one when an archon refused to retire at the end of his year of office. Solon had ended the monopoly of the office by the Well-born, opening it to all who satisfied a property requirement: we must assume that some non-aristocrats were trying to exercise their newly acquired right and that the Well-born were trying to prevent them from doing so. The solution finally adopted is problematic. Where the Athenian Constitution *writes of ten archons, we ought perhaps to think of the ten men elected to the short list of candidates in each tribe; the beginning of his work attributed to Ion a division of the populace into Farmers and Workers for the People (see p. 39), but except in this passage there is no sign of those classes in the historical period, and a simpler rule that in future half of the short list should be drawn from the Well-born and half should not has perhaps been wrongly elaborated.*

The remainder of chapter 13 leads up to the tyranny of Pisistratus by describing and attempting to explain the division of Attica into three locally based factions. Herodotus similarly mentions the factions before the tyranny (I.59), but his is not the source of the account given here; Plutarch's Solon has an account similar to the one given here, placed before the appointment of Solon as archon (13), as well as mentioning the factions in connection with the rise of Pisistratus (29); but almost certainly this particular grouping was a short-lived phenomenon belonging to the time of Pisistratus's rise to prominence.

13

(1) For these reasons Solon went on his travels. In his absence the city continued in a state of turmoil. For four years the peace was kept, but in the fifth [590/89] the strife prevented the appointment of an archon; and again in the fifth year from that [586/5] there was no archon for the same reason. (2) Then, after the same lapse of time again, Damasias was appointed archon [582/1]: he remained in office for two years and two months, until he was removed from his office by force. Then on account of their strife the Athenians resolved to appoint ten archons, five from the Well-born, three from the rustics and two from the Workers for the People, and these held office for the year after Damasias. This makes it clear that it was the archon who wielded the greatest power: we see that that was the office over which strife always arose. (3) In general the Athenians remained in an unhealthy state in their relations with one another: some had the cancellation of debts as the origin and explanation of their discontent, since they had been impoverished by it; others were discontented with the constitution, because of the great change that had been made; others were motivated by personal rivalry. (4) There were three factions: one the men of the coast, led by Megacles son of Alcmeon, whose particular objective seemed to be the middle form of constitution; another the men of the plain, whose aim was oligarchy, and who were led by Lycurgus; and the third, the men of the Diacria, whose leader was Pisistratus, a man who seemed most inclined to democracy. (5) Ranked with this last faction were the men deprived of debts due to them, dis-

contented because of the hardship resulting from this, and those who were not of pure Athenian descent, because of their fear: this is confirmed by the fact that after the overthrow of the tyrants the Athenians held a review of the citizen body, because many men were taking a share in political rights though not entitled to do so. The members of each faction took their name from the region in which they farmed.

F THE TYRANNY (Chapters 14-19)

Chapters 14-15 deal with Pisistratus's three seizures of power, the first two followed by his expulsion, but the third establishing him securely as tyrant. The narrative is derived from Herodotus (I.59-64), but chronological details have been added from an Atthis. Chapter 16 is a collection of material on the rule of Pisistratus, fuller than any other account that survives: we do not know whether our author found this collection in one of his sources or had to put it together himself. Chapters 17-18 deal with the sons of Pisistratus, and with the murder of one of them, Hipparchus, by Harmodius and Aristogiton. The Athenian Constitution follows Herodotus (V.55-61, cf. VI.123) and Thucydides (VI.54-9, cf. I.20) in their protest against what had become standard doctrine in Athens, that the murder of Hipparchus had ended the tyranny, but has its own eccentricity in amalgamating two of Pisistratus's sons as one man known by two names and making it this man rather than Hipparchus whose love for Harmodius was the cause of the trouble. Chapter 19, on the expulsion of Hippias and the ending of the tyranny, is based on Herodotus once more (V.62-5); but again chronological data have been added, and on the part played by Delphi Herodotus's story of oracular pressure is combined with a later version in which money raised for rebuilding the temple was spent on hiring mercenaries.

Herodotus's narrative indicates that the first two periods of tyranny were both short; after the second Pisistratus was in exile for ten years; and his final seizure of power is linked with the Persian defeat of Croesus of Lydia, in 546/5; after that the tyranny lasted for thirty-six years, the murder of Hipparchus occurring four years before the expulsion of Hippias. The chronological data in the papyrus text of the Athenian Constitution *are not wholly consistent, but consistency can be obtained if we correct the figure in 14.4 and that for the total duration of the tyranny in 19.6: the result is the series of dates given in this translation, which makes each of the first two periods of tyranny last several years (despite the contrary indications repeated from Herodotus) and the third seizure of power fall in 536/5. Probably these dates where they conflict with Herodotus are wrong: Pisistratus's first coup was in 561/0, his second was in 557/6 or 556/5, and on each of these occasions he held power for a few months only; his third coup was in 546/5; the later dates in the series are correct.*

14

(1) Pisistratus seemed most inclined to democracy, and won high distinction in the war against Megara. He wounded himself, and persuaded the people that this had been done by his opponents and he should be given a bodyguard; the proposal was made by Aristion. Pisistratus took the men called club-bearers, and with their aid rose against the people and seized the Acropolis, in the thirty-second year after the enactment of the laws, the archonship of Comeas [561/0]. (2) It is said that when he asked for a bodyguard Solon spoke against it, and claimed to be wiser than some and braver than others – that is, wiser than those who failed to realize that Pisistratus was aiming at tyranny, and braver than those who realized but kept quiet about it. When what he said failed to persuade the Athenians, he displayed his arms in front of his door, and said that he had helped his country as far as he could (by then he was a very old man) and called on the others to do likewise. (3) The appeal which Solon made at that time achieved nothing; but Pisistratus on obtaining power administered public affairs more like a citizen than like a tyrant. However, before his rule had taken root, the supporters of Megacles and of Lycurgus combined to expel him, in the sixth year after his first seizure of power, the archonship of Hegesias [556/5]. (4) In the fifth year after that [552/1] Megacles, who was doing badly in the party rivalry, made an offer of support to Pisistratus again, on condition that Pisistratus should marry his

daughter, and reinstated him in a primitive and over-simple manner. He circulated a rumour that Athena was reinstating Pisistratus; and he found a tall and impressive woman called Phye (from the deme of Paeania according to Herodotus [I.60], but a Thracian garland-seller from Collytus according to some writers), dressed her up to resemble Athena, and brought her in with Pisistratus. Pisistratus rode in a chariot with the woman at his side, and the people in the city worshipped and received him with awe.

15

(1) Such was Pisistratus's first return. After this he was expelled for the second time, about the seventh year after his return [546/5]: he did not retain power long, but because of his refusal to have intercourse with Megacles' daughter he became afraid of the two parties and withdrew. (2) First he settled in the region of the Thermaic Gulf at the place called Rhaecelus; from there he proceeded to the district about Pangaeum, where he enriched himself and hired soldiers; then he went to Eretria. It was only in the eleventh year [536/5] that he tried to recover his rule by force, with the support of many others, in particular the Thebans, Lygdamis of Naxos, and the cavalry who controlled the state at Eretria. (3) After winning the battle at Pallenis he occupied the city, deprived the people of their arms, and this time secured the tyranny firmly. Also he captured Naxos and installed Lygdamis as its ruler. (4) He deprived the people of their arms in the following manner. He held an armed parade in the Theseum, tried to address the assembled people, and spoke for a short time. When they said they could not hear him, he told them to go up to the entrance gate of the Acropolis, so that he could make himself better heard. While he took up time with his harangue, men who had been instructed to do this took the arms, shut them up in the buildings near the Theseum, and came and signalled to Pisistratus. (5) When he had finished the rest of his speech, he told the people what had been done with their arms, saying that they should not be startled or disheartened but should go and attend to their private affairs, and that he would take care of all public affairs.

16

(1) That is how Pisistratus's tyranny was established from the beginning, and those are the changes which it underwent. (2) As has been said above, Pisistratus administered the city's affairs moderately, and more like a citizen than like a tyrant. In general he was humane, mild, and forgiving to wrongdoers, and in particular he lent money to those who were in difficulties, to support their work, so that they could continue to maintain themselves by farming. (3) He did this for two reasons: so that they should spend their time not in the city but scattered about the countryside, and so that they should have reasonable means of subsistence, and should concentrate on their private affairs and have neither the desire nor the leisure to take an interest in public affairs. (4) At the same time this resulted in an increase in his own revenues from the thorough working of the land: for he levied a tithe on the produce. (5) For this reason again he instituted the deme justices, and he himself often went out into the country to inspect and to reconcile disputants, so that they should not come down to the city and neglect their work. (6) It is said that when Pisistratus was on one of these tours there occurred the incident involving the man on Mount Hymettus who was farming what was afterwards called the tax-free site. Pisistratus saw him digging and working at what was nothing but rock, and in amazement told his attendant to ask him what he got from the site. 'Nothing but evil and pain,' he said, 'and of this evil and pain a tithe has to go to Pisistratus.' The man gave his reply without recognizing him; and Pisistratus, pleased at his forthrightness and his industry, made him free from all taxes. (7) Pisistratus gave the masses no trouble in other respects during his rule, but always maintained peace and saw that all was quiet. For that reason it was often said that the tyranny of Pisistratus was the age of Cronus; for afterwards, when his sons took over, the regime became much more cruel. (8) Most important of all the things mentioned was his democratic and humane manner. In other respects he was willing to administer everything according to the laws, not giving himself any advantage; and on one occasion, when he was summoned before the Areopagus on a homicide charge, he attended to make his defence – but the prosecutor took fright and defaulted. (9) Consequently he remained

in power for a long time, and when he was expelled he easily recovered his position. He had many supporters both among the notables and among the ordinary people: he won over the notables by his friendly dealings with them, and the people by his help for their private concerns, and he behaved honourably to both. (10) At that time the Athenians' laws about tyrants were mild, in particular the one relating to the setting-up of a tyranny. The law ran: 'This is an ordinance and tradition of the Athenians: if men rise with the aim of tyranny, or if any one joins in setting up a tyranny, he and his issue shall be without rights.'

17

(1) Pisistratus grew old in his rule and died from an illness, in the archonship of Philoneos [528/7]: he had lived thirty-three years from his first seizure of the tyranny, spending nineteen of those years in power and the rest of the time in exile. (2) It is therefore palpable nonsense when people say that he was loved by Solon and was a general in the war against Megara for Salamis: the chronology does not allow it, if you reckon up the life of each man and the archonship in which each died. (3) On the death of Pisistratus his sons took over the regime, and continued the management of affairs in the same way. He had two sons by his wedded wife, Hippias and Hipparchus, and two by the Argive woman, Iophon and Hegesistratus (the latter had the additional name Thessalus). (4) Pisistratus married Timonassa from Argos, the daughter of an Argive called Gorgilus; she had previously been married to Archinus of Ambracia, of the Cypselid family. That was the origin of his friendship with the Argives, and a thousand Argives were brought by Hegesistratus and fought as Pisistratus's allies at the battle of Pallenis. Some say that Pisistratus married Timonassa in his first period of exile; others, when he was first established in power.

18

(1) Hipparchus and Hippias were in control of affairs, on account of their reputation and their age. Hippias, who was the elder and was public-spirited and sensible in character, was at the head of

the regime. Hipparchus was childish, amorous and fond of the arts; it was he who had invited the circle of Anacreon, Simonides and the other poets to Athens. (2) Thessalus was much younger, and was bold and insolent in his way of life; and he was the origin of all their misfortunes. He fell in love with Harmodius, but failed to win his affection; he could not suppress his anger at this, but gave various bitter indications of it; and, finally, when Harmodius's sister was going to serve as basket-bearer at the Panathenaea [in 514/3], he prevented it, and infuriated Harmodius by casting aspersions on him as effeminate. So Harmodius and Aristogiton did the deed, and they had many supporters. (3) When they were waiting to catch Hippias on the Acropolis at the Panathenaea (it was his function to receive the procession, and Hipparchus's to dispatch it), they saw one of the men involved in the plot meeting Hippias in a friendly manner, and thought he was turning informer. Wanting to achieve something before they were arrested, they went down from the Acropolis, and acted without waiting for the others: they killed Hipparchus as he was organizing the procession by the Leocoreum. This ruined the whole plot. (4) Harmodius was killed immediately by the bodyguard. Aristogiton was caught afterwards and tortured for a long time, and under pressure he denounced many men who were of noble birth and were friends of the tyrants. (It had been impossible to find any immediate clue to the plot; and the story that Hippias made the members of the procession stand apart from their arms and caught the men carrying daggers is untrue: the procession was not armed at that date, but this was a subsequent institution of the democracy.) (5) Democratic writers say that Aristogiton denounced friends of the tyrants deliberately, so that the tyranny should simultaneously be polluted and weakened by the killing of men who were both innocent and friendly; but others say that he was not inventing it but that the men whom he named actually were involved in the plot. (6) In the end, when nothing that he did would provoke the authorities to kill him, he promised to name many more men, persuaded Hippias to give him his right hand as a pledge, and then, on taking it, reviled Hippias for giving his hand to his brother's murderer. This enraged Hippias and, unable to control his anger, he pulled out his dagger and killed Aristogiton.

(1) After this the tyranny became much more cruel. Hippias took revenge for his brother's death, with many executions and expulsions, and became suspicious and bitter towards everyone. (2) About the fourth year after Hipparchus's death, since things were in a bad way in the city, he began to fortify Munichia with a view to moving there; but while the work was in progress he was expelled by king Cleomenes of Sparta. A whole series of oracles had commanded the Spartans to put an end to the tyranny, for the following reason. (3) The Athenian exiles, chief among whom were the Alcmaeonids, were unable to bring about their return on their own, in spite of several attempts. Among their other failures was one when they fortified Lipsydrium in the countryside below Parnes, and were joined by some men from the city, but the tyrants besieged them and drove them out. After this disaster they used to sing in their drinking-songs:

> Alas, Lipsydrium, betrayer of comrades,
> What men you lost,
> Good warriors and well-born,
> Who showed then what stock they came of.

(4) After they had failed in everything else, the Alcmaeonids obtained the contract to build the temple at Delphi, and so acquired ample funds to enlist the Spartans' help. Whenever the Spartans consulted the oracle, the priestess always commanded them to liberate Athens, and eventually she persuaded the Spartan citizens, in spite of their ties of hospitality with the Pisistratids. Another factor which contributed no less to the Spartans' decision was the friendship of the Pisistratids for Argos. (5) First the Spartans sent Anchimolus, who took a force by sea; but Cineas of Thessaly came to support Hippias with a thousand cavalry, and Anchimolus was defeated and killed. Angry at this, they sent king Cleomenes by land with a larger force: he defeated the Thessalian cavalry when they tried to prevent him from entering Attica; and then he confined Hippias within what is called the Pelargic wall, and with support from the Athenians laid siege to him. (6) As the siege continued, the sons of the Pisistratids were caught when they were being sent out to safety,

after which the Pisistratids came to terms to secure their children's safety, and in five days evacuated their possessions and handed over the Acropolis to the Athenians. This was in the archonship of Harpactides [511/0]: the Pisistratids had held the tyranny for about seventeen years after their father's death, and the total length of the tyranny, including their father's rule, was thirty-six years.

G FROM CLEISTHENES' REFORMS TO XERXES' INVASION (Chapters 20–22)

Chapter 20 begins with a narrative, derived from Herodotus (V.66–73), of the rivalry between Cleisthenes and Isagoras, the initial success of Isagoras (probably his election as archon), Cleisthenes' bid for popular support, and Isagoras's unsuccessful invocation of Cleomenes of Sparta. To round off his account of the success of Cleisthenes the Alcmaeonid, our author then reverts to the part played by the Alcmaeonids in the ending of the tyranny. In chapter 21 he turns to a different source, for a more detailed account of Cleisthenes' reorganization of the citizen body than was available in Herodotus: a resolution of 411, quoted in 29.3, calls for the consultation of Cleisthenes' laws, but it is not certain whether his laws like Solon's did survive to be consulted by later politicians and historians. Chapter 22 begins by summing up Cleisthenes' dispensation, as more democratic than that of Solon. Then follows a list of politically significant events down to 480: the introduction of an oath for the council of five hundred; the annual election of ten generals; the use of ostracism to remove several prominent men from Athens in the 480s; a change in the appointment of the archons; Themistocles' use of surplus money from the silver mines to enlarge the Athenian navy; and, in response to the Persian invasion, the recall of those who had been ostracized and the introduction of a rule that men ostracized in future should keep clear of the Persians. Much of the material in chapters 21–2 is to be found in no other surviving text: this information with its series of dates is probably derived from an Atthis, and we have reason to believe that the Atthis used was that of Androtion (see note on 22.3–4).

20

(1) When the tyranny had been overthrown, strife broke out between Isagoras son of Tisander, a friend of the tyrants, and Cleisthenes of the Alcmaeonid family. As Cleisthenes was getting the worse of the party struggle, he attached the people to his following, by proposing to give political power to the masses. (2) Isagoras then fell behind in power, so he called back Cleomenes, with whom he had a tie of hospitality, and since it appeared that the Alcmaeonids were among those who were under a curse, persuaded Cleomenes to join him in driving out the accursed. (3) Cleisthenes withdrew; and Cleomenes came with a few men and solemnly expelled seven hundred Athenian households. After doing this he tried to dissolve the council and make Isagoras and three hundred of his friends masters of the city. However, the council resisted and the common people gathered in force; the supporters of Cleomenes and Isagoras fled to the Acropolis; the people settled down and besieged them for two days, but on the third made a truce to release Cleomenes and all the men with him, and recalled Cleisthenes and the other exiles. (4) Thus the people obtained control of affairs, and Cleisthenes became leader and champion of the people. The Alcmaeonids bore the greatest responsibility for the expulsion of the tyrants, and had persisted in opposition to them for most of the time. (5) Even earlier, Cedon of the Alcmaeonids had attacked the tyrants, and so he too was celebrated in drinking-songs:

> Pour to Cedon also, steward, and forget him not,
> If wine is to be poured to valiant men.

21

(1) For these reasons the people placed their trust in Cleisthenes. Then, as champion of the masses, in the fourth year after the overthrow of the tyrants, the archonship of Isagoras [508/7], (2) he first distributed all the citizens through ten tribes instead of the old four, wanting to mix them up so that more men should have a share in the running of the state. This is the origin of the saying 'Don't judge by tribes', addressed to those who want to inquire into a man's ancestry. (3) Next he made the council a body of five hundred instead

of four hundred, fifty from each tribe (previously there had been a hundred from each old tribe). He refused to divide the Athenians into twelve tribes, to avoid allocating them according to the already existing thirds: the four tribes were divided into twelve thirds, and if he had used them he would not have succeeded in mixing up the people. (4) He divided the land of Attica by demes into thirty parts – ten parts in the city region, ten in the coast and ten in the inland – and he called these parts thirds, and allotted three to each tribe in such a way that each tribe should have a share in all the regions. He made the men living in each deme fellow-demesmen of one another, so that they should not use their fathers' names and make it obvious who were the new citizens but should be named after their demes: this is why the Athenians still call themselves after their demes. (5) He instituted demarchs, with the same responsibilities as the old *naucrari*; for he made the demes take the place of the *naucrariae*. He named some of the demes after their localities, and some after their founders (not all founders of the demes were known any longer). (6) He left the clans, brotherhoods and priesthoods each to retain their traditional privileges. He appointed ten eponymous heroes for the tribes, chosen by the Delphic priestess from a pre-selected list of a hundred founding heroes.

22

(1) When this had been accomplished, the constitution was much more democratic than that of Solon. Many of Solon's laws had been consigned to oblivion by the tyranny, through not being used, and Cleisthenes enacted other new laws in his bid for popular support, among them the law about ostracism. (2) First, in the eighth year after this settlement [501/0], the archonship of Hermocreon, the Athenians imposed on the council of five hundred the oath which it still swears today. Then they appointed the generals by tribes, one from each tribe; but the leader of the whole army was the polemarch. (3) In the twelfth year after this, the archonship of Phaenippus [490/89], they won the battle of Marathon. They waited two years after their victory, and then [488/7], now that the people were confident, they used for the first time the law about ostracism: this had been enacted through suspicion of men in a powerful

position, because Pisistratus from being popular leader and general had made himself tyrant. (4) The first man to be ostracized was one of his relatives, Hipparchus son of Charmus, of Collytus: it was because of him in particular that Cleisthenes had enacted the law, since he wanted to drive Hipparchus out. The Athenians, with the tolerance normally shown by the people, had allowed those friends of the tyrants who had not joined in their crimes during the disturbances to continue living in the city, and Hipparchus was the leader and champion of these. (5) Immediately afterwards, in the next year, the archonship of Telesinus [487/6], for the first time since the tyranny the nine archons were appointed by lot on a tribal basis, from a short list of five hundred elected by the members of the demes: all the archons before this were elected. Also Megacles son of Hippocrates, of Alopece, was ostracized. (6) The Athenians continued for three years to ostracize the friends of the tyrants, on account of whom the law had been enacted; but after that, in the fourth year [485/4], they took to removing anyone else who seemed too powerful: the first man unconnected with the tyranny to be ostracized was Xanthippus son of Ariphron. (7) In the third year after that, the archonship of Nicodemus [483/2], when the mines at Maronea were discovered and the city had a surplus of one hundred talents from the workings, some men proposed that the money should be distributed to the people, but Themistocles prevented this. He refused to say what he would do with the money, but urged the Athenians to lend the hundred richest citizens one talent each: if they were satisfied with the way in which the money was spent, it should be put down to the city's account, but if not, the money should be reclaimed from those to whom it had been lent. When he had obtained the money on these terms, he had a hundred triremes built, each of the hundred men taking the responsibility for one; and with these ships the battle of Salamis was fought against the barbarians. At this time Aristides son of Lysimachus was ostracized. (8) In the third year [481/0], the archonship of Hypsichides, all those who had been ostracized were recalled, on account of Xerxes' invasion: and for the future it was resolved that anyone who was ostracized should live within the limits of Geraestus and Scyllaeum, or else was to be absolutely outlawed.

H THE MID FIFTH CENTURY (Chapters 23–8)

The Athenian Constitution's *chapters on the mid fifth century are disappointing: they contain a good deal of politically biased anecdote and comment, and comparatively little solid material, and they do not present a coherent account of the period. Thucydides in reviewing the growth of Athenian power complained that previous writers had neglected this period (I.97), and our author probably found it hard to amass material on it; he seems to have had recourse to a variety of sources, and to have had difficulty in putting together what he found in them.*

At the beginning of chapter 23 we read that after the Persian Wars the growth of democracy was halted and the council of the Areopagus played a dominant role; but from the second sentence of section 2 to the end of chapter 24 we encounter Aristides and Themistocles as joint champions of the people, Aristides' organization of the Delian League, the conversion of the League into an empire and the maintenance of large numbers of Athenian citizens on the revenue from the empire: the same awkward combination of an anti-democratic and a democratic sequel to the Persian Wars is to be found in Aristotle's Politics *(V. 1304a). 25.1–2 harks back to the dominance of the Areopagus, and then gives an account of Ephialtes' reform of the Areopagus, from the reformer's point of view. This is followed in 25.3–4 by an anecdote of Themistocles' involvement with Ephialtes: the anecdote is chronologically impossible, and there is only one other mention of it in an ancient text (an introduction to Isocrates' Areopagitic); like the 'Constitution of Draco' in chapter 4 (see p. 42), this was probably absent from the original edition of the* Athenian Constitution *but was subsequently added to the text.*

Chapter 26 begins with a belated and unflattering introduction of Cimon, who in fact built up the Delian League in the 470s and 460s, and was ostracized when he opposed Ephialtes; in the remainder of the chapter we have a sober account of three constitutional changes of the 450s, probably (like the similar material in chapters 21–2) derived from an Atthis. Chapter 27 is a rambling and hostile treatment of Pericles: a favourable picture could have been obtained, but was not, from Thucydides (especially II.65).

Chapter 28, opening with the remark that after Pericles' death things became much worse (from an aristocratic point of view), proceeds to give a schematic list of paired aristocratic and democratic leaders to the end of the fifth century, and concludes by praising the last three aristocratic leaders: at various points the list fails to match our author's own narrative, so presumably he did not compile it himself but took it over from an earlier writer. Apart from the comments on some of the later figures in this list, we are given no material at all to bridge the gap between Pericles' death and the oligarchic revolution of 411 (which follows in chapters 29–33).

23

(1) Up to this point there had been a gradual development and increase in the city and in the democracy. After the Persian Wars, however, the council of the Areopagus recovered its strength and administered the city. It acquired its predominance not by any formal decision but through being responsible for the battle of Salamis. When the generals were unable to handle the crisis, and proclaimed that each man should save himself, the Areopagus provided money, gave the men eight drachmae each, and enabled them to embark on the ships. (2) For this reason the Athenians bowed to its authority, and the city was well governed at this time. During this period they trained themselves for war, gained a good reputation among the Greeks, and acquired the leadership at sea despite the opposition of the Spartans. (3) The champions of the people at this time were Aristides son of Lysimachus and Themistocles son of Neocles: Themistocles practised the military arts, while Aristides was skilled in the political arts and was outstanding among his contemporaries for his uprightness, so the Athenians used the first as a general and the second as an adviser. (4) The two men were jointly responsible for the rebuilding of the walls, in spite of being personal opponents; and it was Aristides who saw that the Spartans had gained a bad reputation because of Pausanias and urged the Ionians to break away from the Spartan alliance. (5) For that reason it was he who made the first assessment of tribute for the cities, in the third year after the battle of Salamis, the archonship of

Timosthenes [478/7], and who swore the oaths to the Ionians that they should have the same enemies and friends, to confirm which they sank lumps of iron in the sea.

24

(1) After this, now that the city was confident and a large amount of money had been collected, Aristides advised the Athenians to assert their leadership, and to leave the fields and live in the city: there would be maintenance for all, some on campaign, some on guard duty, others attending to public affairs; and by living in this way they would secure their leadership. (2) The Athenians were persuaded. They took control of the empire, and became more domineering in their treatment of the allies, apart from Chios, Lesbos and Samos: these they kept as guardians of the empire, accepting their existing constitutions and allowing them to retain the subjects over whom they ruled. (3) In accordance with Aristides' proposal, they provided ample maintenance for the common people, so that more than twenty thousand men were supported from the tribute, the taxes and the allies. There were 6,000 jurors; 1,600 archers, and also 1,200 cavalry; the council of 500; 500 guards of the dockyards, and also 50 guards on the Acropolis; about 700 internal officials and about 700 overseas. In addition to these, when the Athenians subsequently organized their military affairs, they had 2,500 hoplites; 20 guard ships; other ships sent out for the tribute, carrying 2,000 men appointed by lot; also the town hall; orphans; and guardians of prisoners. All these were financed from public funds.

25

(1) That is how maintenance for the people came into being. For about seventeen years after the Persian Wars the constitution in which the Areopagus was dominant persisted, though it gradually declined. As the masses increased, Ephialtes son of Sophonides became champion of the people, a man who appeared to be uncorrupt and upright in political matters. He attacked the council of the Areopagus. (2) First he eliminated many of its members, bringing them to trial for their conduct in office. Then in the archon-

ship of Conon [462/1] he took away from the council all the accretions which gave it its guardianship of the constitution, giving some to the council of five hundred and some to the people and the jurycourts. (3) Themistocles shared in the responsibility for this achievement. He was a member of the Areopagus, and was about to be tried for collaboration with the Persians. Wanting to bring about the downfall of the Areopagus, he said to Ephialtes that the council was about to make away with him, and to the members that he would show them men who were conspiring to overthrow the constitution. He brought some men chosen from the council to the place where Ephialtes was, as if to show them the conspirators assembled, and engaged in earnest conversation with them. Ephialtes on seeing this took fright and, wearing only his undergarment, sat as a suppliant at the altar. (4) Everyone was amazed at what had happened. Afterwards Ephialtes and Themistocles attacked the Areopagus at a meeting of the council of five hundred, and then in the assembly in the same way, and persisted until they had taken away its power. Ephialtes too was removed by assassination not long afterwards, through the agency of Aristodicus of Tanagra.

26

(1) In this way the council of the Areopagus was deprived of its responsibility. Afterwards the constitution was further slackened through the men who devoted themselves eagerly to demagogy. At this time it happened that the better sort had no leader, but their champion was Cimon son of Miltiades, a youngish man who had only recently turned to public affairs. In addition, many had been killed in war: at that time military service was based on selective conscription, and the generals who commanded were men lacking in experience of war but honoured because of their forebears' reputations; thus it regularly happened that two or three thousand of the men sent out were killed, and the casualties fell on the better sort of both the ordinary people and the wealthy. (2) In other respects the Athenians in their administration did not abide by the laws as they had done before, but at first they did not interfere with the appointment of the nine archons. However, in the sixth year after Ephialtes' death they decided that the rankers should be admitted

to the short list from which lots were drawn for the nine archons, and Mnesithides was the first of these to hold office [457/6]. Previously all the archons had been from the cavalry and the five-hundred-bushel class, and the rankers had held only the routine offices, except when some stipulation of the law was disregarded. (3) In the fifth year after that, the archonship of Lysicrates [453/2], the thirty justices called deme justices were instituted again. (4) In the third year after that, under Antidotus [451/0], on account of the large number of citizens it was decided on the proposal of Pericles that a man should not be a member of the citizen body unless both his parents were Athenians.

27

(1) After this Pericles took on the leadership of the people; he had first distinguished himself when, as a young man, he prosecuted Cimon in the examination after his generalship. The constitution now became still more democratic: Pericles took away some of the powers of the Areopagus, and above all turned the city in the direction of naval power, so that the common people grew confident and increasingly attracted to themselves complete control of the state. (2) In the forty-ninth year after the battle of Salamis, the archonship of Pythodorus [432/1], the Peloponnesian War broke out. During the war the people were shut up in the city, grew accustomed to earning stipends on campaign, and – partly intentionally, partly not – chose to administer public affairs themselves. (3) Moreover, Pericles was the first man to provide payment for jury service, as a political measure to counter the generosity of Cimon. Cimon was as rich as a tyrant: he performed the public liturgies lavishly; and he maintained many of his fellow-demesmen, for any man of Laciadae who wished could go to him each day and obtain his basic needs, and all his land was unfenced, so that anyone who wished could enjoy the fruit. (4) Pericles' property was insufficient for this kind of service. He was therefore advised by Damonides of Oe (who seems to have been the originator of most of Pericles' measures, and for that reason was subsequently ostracized) that since he was less well supplied with private property he should give the people their own property; and so he devised payment for the jurors. Some

people allege that it was as a result of this that the courts deteriorated, since it was always the ordinary people rather than the better sort who were eager to be picked for jury service. (5) After this judicial corruption began. The way was first shown by Anytus after he had served as general at Pylos: he was brought to trial for losing Pylos, and escaped by bribing the jury.

28

(1) While Pericles was champion of the people the constitution was not in too bad a state, but after his death it became much worse. It was then that the people first took a champion who was not of good repute among the better sort, whereas previously it was always men of the better sort who were popular leaders. (2) To begin at the beginning, Solon was the first champion of the people; the second was Pisistratus, while Lycurgus was champion of the well-born and notable; after the overthrow of the tyranny came Cleisthenes, of the Alcmaeonid family, and he had no opponent, since Isagoras's party was expelled. After this Xanthippus was champion of the people and Miltiades of the notables; then Themistocles and Aristides respectively; after them Ephialtes was champion of the people and Cimon son of Miltiades champion of the wealthy; then Pericles was champion of the people and Thucydides, a relative of Cimon, champion of the others. (3) After Pericles' death the distinguished were championed by Nicias, who died in Sicily, and the people by Cleon son of Cleaenetus: Cleon, it seems, more than anyone else corrupted the people by his wild impulses, and was the first man who, when on the platform, shouted, uttered abuse and made speeches with his clothes hitched up, while everyone else spoke in an orderly manner. Next, after them, Theramenes son of Hagnon was champion of the others and Cleophon the lyre-maker champion of the people. Cleophon was the first man to provide the two-obol grant: for a while it continued to be paid, then it was abolished by Callicrates of Paeania, after he had first promised to add another obol to the two. Both Cleophon and Callicrates were subsequently condemned to death by the Athenians: the masses generally come to hate those who have led them on to do anything wrong, particularly if they have deceived them. (4) Since Cleophon there

has been an unending succession of popular leaders whose chief desire has been to be outrageous and to gratify the masses, looking only to considerations of the moment. (5) It appears that the best of the Athenian politicians after the older ones were Nicias, Thucydides and Theramenes. As far as Nicias and Thucydides are concerned, almost everyone agrees that they were not only gentlemen but were public-spirited and behaved like fathers towards the whole city; but the verdict on Theramenes is disputed, because in his time there was constitutional upheaval. However, the judgement of those who are not superficial critics is that he did not destroy all regimes, as his detractors allege, but supported all as long as they did nothing unlawful (since he was able to take part in politics under all regimes, as a good citizen should), but when they broke the law did not acquiesce but incurred their enmity.

I THE FOUR HUNDRED AND THE FIVE THOUSAND
(Chapters 29–33)

We have two accounts of the Athenian revolutions of 411. Thucydides wrote not long after the events: he was in exile, and so free from involvement in the events but dependent on what others told him; he sets the events in an atmosphere of intrigue, intimidation and distrust, and frequently contrasts the motives publicly professed by the actors with those by which he believes they were really activated. The Athenian Constitution, *written almost a century later, gives an account devoted largely to technical details and the formalities of the constitutional changes, which has the effect of showing the oligarchs in a comparatively favourable light. Thucydides' account was used by our author; most of his other material is derived ultimately from documents, quoted possibly in self-defence by Antiphon or one of the other extremists when put on trial (Antiphon's defence was celebrated), or possibly in the* Atthis *of Androtion (whose father Andron was responsible for bringing Antiphon and others to trial under the intermediate regime of 411/0).*

The events leading up to the oligarchic revolution are narrated in detail by Thucydides (VIII.45–66), mentioned briefly at the beginning of chapter 29 of the Athenian Constitution: *the democracy could no longer claim that it was making a success of the Peloponnesian War; Athens had squandered her resources and had provoked Persia, while Sparta had gained access to Persia's comparatively unlimited resources; Alcibiades (never mentioned in the Athenian Constitution), exiled from Athens earlier, had now fallen out with Sparta and was trying to return to Athens and claiming that he could divert Persian support to the Athenian side. The remainder of chapter 29 deals with the appointment of a drafting committee and with the assembly which formally adopted an oligarchic constitution: there are serious discrepancies between this account and that of Thucydides (VIII.67–71), and probably neither tells the whole truth. Chapters 30–31 quote two constitutional documents, one 'for the future' and one 'for the immediate crisis'. Probably the assembly of 29.4–5 adopted an oligarchic constitution in principle and appointed a new committee to work out the details; members of the committee disagreed on the kind of oligarchy that they wanted, and the plans of the extremists were embodied in the 'immediate' constitution, while theorists who wanted a different form of government were allowed to advance theirs as a constitution 'for the future'; these drafts were approved not by an assembly (despite 32.1) but only by the Four Hundred. Chapter 32 gives precise dates, repeats from Thucydides the names of the leading oligarchs, and ends with the absolute rule of the Four Hundred and their unsuccessful attempt to make peace with Sparta.*

Having overthrown the democracy, the oligarchs disagreed among themselves, and they neither achieved a peace settlement nor prosecuted the war successfully. Chapter 33, based on Thucydides (VIII.89–98), mentions Athens' defeat in a naval battle off Eretria, the deposition of the Four Hundred, and the setting up of an intermediate regime, for which our author echoes Thucydides' approval. Thucydides' history ends in the autumn of 411; other evidence suggests that the intermediate regime lasted until the summer of 410, when the full democracy was restored.

29

(1) As long as the war was evenly balanced, the Athenians preserved the democracy. But when, after the disaster in Sicily, the Spartan

side was strengthened through its alliance with the Persian king, they were compelled to interfere with the democracy and set up the constitution of the Four Hundred: the speech introducing the decree was made by Melobius, and the motion stood in the name of Pythodorus of Anaphlystus. The many were persuaded especially by the thought that the King would be more likely to fight on their side if they based the constitution on a few men. (2) Pythodorus's decree was as follows. 'The people shall elect, in addition to the ten commissioners already in existence, a further twenty from the citizens over forty years old; these shall take an oath to draft such proposals as they believe to be in the best interests of the city, and shall draft proposals with a view to the city's safety. It shall be open also to anyone else who wishes to submit proposals, so that the committee may choose the best of all the proposals that are made.' (3) Clitophon moved that in other respects Pythodorus's proposal should be followed, but that the men elected should also search out the traditional laws which Cleisthenes had enacted when he set up the democracy, so that they might consider these too and deliberate for the best – his point being that Cleisthenes' constitution was not populist but very much like Solon's. (4) The men who were elected proposed first that it should be obligatory for the *prytanes* to put to the vote all proposals that should be made for the safety of Athens. Then they suspended the prosecutions for illegal proposal, the denunciations and the summonses, so that those Athenians who wished might be free to deliberate on the matters laid before them; if on account of these matters anyone imposed a penalty, made a summons or brought a case into court, he should be liable to indication and delivery before the generals, and the generals should hand him over to the Eleven to be put to death. (5) After this they organized the constitution in the following way. It should not be permitted to spend Athens' revenues for any purpose other than the war; and all officials should serve without stipends for the duration of the war, apart from the nine archons and whatever *prytanes* there might be, who should each receive three obols a day. Otherwise the whole control of the state should be entrusted to the Athenians best able to serve with their persons and their wealth, being not less than five thousand in number, for the duration of the war: this body of men should have full power to make treaties with whoever they wished. Ten men over forty years old should be chosen from each tribe, should swear an oath over sacred victims, and should draw up a register of the Five Thousand.

30

(1) Those are the proposals made by the elected committee. When they had been ratified, the Five Thousand elected from their own number a hundred men to draw up the details of the constitution, and the men who were elected drew up and submitted the following. (2) The men over thirty years old should form the council year by year, without stipend; from their number should be appointed the generals, the nine archons, the sacred recorder, the regimental commanders, the cavalry commanders, the squadron commanders, the garrison officers, ten treasurers of the sacred funds of the goddess Athena and of the Other Gods, twenty *hellenotamiae* to administer their own treasury and also all other secular funds, ten *hieropoei* and ten overseers. All these were to be elected from a larger number chosen by election from the current council; all the remaining officials were to be appointed by lot and not from the current council; the *hellenotamiae* who administered funds should not be included in the council. (3) For the future four councils should be formed from the age-group stated above, and one of these four sections should be picked by lot to hold office as the current council. The men who had not yet reached the required age should be distributed among the four divisions; the hundred registrars should distribute themselves and the rest of the Five Thousand in four sections as evenly as possible. Lots should be drawn, and the council should hold office for a year. (4) The council should deliberate as seemed best to them about finance, to keep funds safe and spend them for necessary purposes, and as best they could about other matters. If they wanted to deliberate with a larger number, each member should invite one other man of his choice from the same age-group. Meetings of the council should be held every fifth day, unless more were needed. (5) The council should be convened by the nine archons; the results of the voting should be determined by five men appointed by lot from the council, one of these being picked by lot each day to put motions to the vote. The five men should draw lots among those wishing to appear before

the council, first on religious matters, secondly for heralds, thirdly for embassies, fourthly on other matters. Matters concerning the war should be dealt with whenever necessary, without drawing lots, and for these the generals should be brought in. (6) Any member of the council who failed to come to the council-house at the hour specified should incur a penalty of one drachma for each day, unless he stayed away after applying for leave of absence from the council.

31

(1) The committee drew up that constitution for the future, and the following for the immediate crisis. There should be a council of four hundred in accordance with tradition, forty from each tribe, appointed from a short list elected by the tribes from men over thirty years old. The council should appoint the officials and draw up the oath which they were to swear, and with regard to the laws, examinations and everything else act as they thought expedient. (2) The Athenians should abide by whatever constitutional laws were enacted, and it should not be permitted to interfere with them or to enact others. For the present the generals should be elected from all the Five Thousand; but when the council had been established it should hold an armed review of the citizens, and elect ten men as generals, and a secretary for them. The men elected should hold office with full power for the coming year, and if they needed anything should deliberate with the council. (3) One cavalry commander and ten squadron commanders should be elected; for the future they were to be appointed by the council in the manner laid down for the appointment of the generals. Apart from the council and the generals, no other official should hold the same office more than once. So that in the future the Four Hundred shall be distributed among the four divisions, when it becomes possible for them to join in deliberation with the rest of the Five Thousand, they are to be assigned to their divisions by the hundred registrars.

32

(1) That is the constitution drawn up by the hundred men who were elected by the Five Thousand: it was ratified by the masses, at an

assembly under the presidency of Aristomachus. Then the council of the archonship of Callias was dissolved before completing its year, on 14 Thargelion, and the Four Hundred were inaugurated on 22 Thargelion (the new council appointed by lot ought to have been inaugurated on 14 Scirophorion). (2) That is how the oligarchy was set up, in the archonship of Callias [412/1], about a hundred years after the expulsion of the tyrants: the men most responsible were Pisander, Antiphon, Phrynichus and Theramenes, men who were well born and appeared outstanding in intelligence and judgement. (3) Under this constitution the Five Thousand were appointed only in name, while the Four Hundred with the powerful ten generals entered the council-house and began ruling the city. They sent envoys to Sparta, to put an end to the war on the terms that each side should retain what it currently possessed, but the Spartans would not agree unless the Athenians were prepared to give up their rule of the sea, so they abandoned the attempt.

33

(1) The constitution of the Four Hundred lasted for about four months, and Mnasilochus from their ranks was archon for about two months in the archonship of Theopompus [411/0], who held office for the remaining ten months. When the Athenians had been defeated in the sea-battle off Eretria, and all Euboea except Oreus was in revolt, they found this misfortune harder to bear than what had gone before, for they had been deriving more benefit from Euboea than from Attica. Then they overthrew the Four Hundred, entrusting affairs to the Five Thousand of the hoplite class and resolving that there should be no stipend for any office. (2) The men most responsible for the overthrow of the Four Hundred were Aristocrates and Theramenes, who were dissatisfied with their conduct because they did everything on their own and referred nothing to the Five Thousand. The Athenians seem to have been well governed at this time, when they were at war and the constitution was based on the hoplites.

J THE THIRTY AND THE TEN (Chapters 34–41.1)

The first sentence of chapter 34 probably refers to the ending of the intermediate regime and the restoration of the democracy, in 410, though some have argued that it is a resumptive sentence harking back to the overthrow of the Four Hundred and that the Athenian Constitution *passes over the ending of the intermediate regime altogether. The remainder of 34.1 briefly mentions the condemnation of the generals after the battle of Arginusae (see Xenophon, Hellenica I.6–7; Diodorus of Sicily, XIII.98–103), and a Spartan peace offer frustrated by Cleophon (Diodorus, XIII.52–3). The condemnation of the generals is inaccurately described, and the peace offer is wrongly dated: probably in this transitional passage between the two periods of oligarchy our author simply wrote what he thought he knew, without checking his facts.*

Then follows a detailed account of the oligarchy set up after Athens' defeat in the Peloponnesian War, and the subsequent restoration of the democracy. We have other accounts, by Xenophon (Hellenica II.3–4), Diodorus (XIV.3–6, 32–3) and Justin (epitome of the history by Pompeius Trogus, V.8–10), the last two from a common source. The Athenian Constitution *seems to have made use of a defence of Theramenes which was used by Xenophon also, but otherwise it goes its own way. Our other sources place the invitation to Sparta to send a garrison, the disarming of the unprivileged Athenians, the killing of Theramenes, and Thrasybulus's occupation of Phyle in that order, but here the order is reversed: the early occupation of Phyle may be correct (and its late position in the other sources a matter of narrative tidiness rather than chronology), but the rearrangement of the other three episodes appears to be a distortion of the truth, made in order to remove Theramenes from the scene before, and to absolve him of any share in the responsibility for, the major offences of the Thirty (but it is not exploited for this purpose in the* Athenian Constitution, *which suppresses the fact that Theramenes was a member of the Thirty). Another eccentricity is the claim that there were two successive boards of Ten after the overthrow of the Thirty, the first hostile to the democrats but the second virtuously favourable to them. As on the revolutions of 411, some of the material peculiar to the* Athenian Constitution *appears to be derived ultimately from official documents. In the main account there is no awkwardness pointing to the combination of material drawn from conflicting sources: nothing is said which could not have been transmitted by one of the 'moderate' leaders of the restored democracy praised in chapter 40. The summary in 41.1, however, conflicts with what has gone before on the dating of the restoration, and writes no longer of moderation and reconciliation but of the victory of the people.*

34

(1) The people soon took away their control of the state. In the sixth year after the overthrow of the Four Hundred, the archonship of Callias of Angele [406/5], the sea-battle of Arginusae was fought. After that, first, the ten generals who had won the battle were all condemned in a single vote, though some had not taken part in the battle and others had lost their own ships and had been saved by other ships: the people were deceived by those who stirred up their anger. Secondly, when the Spartans were willing to evacuate Decelea and make peace on the terms that each side should retain what it currently possessed, some were eager to accept but the masses were not: they were deceived by Cleophon, who prevented them from making peace by going into the assembly drunk and wearing his breastplate, and saying that he would not allow it unless the Spartans surrendered all the cities that they had taken. (2) The Athenians mismanaged affairs then, and not long afterwards they discovered their mistake. In the following year, the archonship of Alexias [405/4], they lost the sea-battle of Aegospotami, and as a result of that Lysander became master of the city, and set up the Thirty in the following manner. (3) Peace had been made on condition that the Athenians should live under their traditional constitution. The democrats tried to preserve the democracy; of the notables those who belonged to the clubs and the exiles who had returned after the peace treaty were eager for oligarchy; those who did not belong to any club and who in other respects seemed inferior to none of the citizens had as their objective the traditional constitution: these last included Archinus, Anytus, Clitophon, Phormisius and many others, but their particular champion was Theramenes.

Lysander gave his support to the oligarchs, and the people were intimidated and compelled to decide in favour of the oligarchy. The author of the decree was Dracontides of Aphidna.

35

(1) In this way the Thirty were established, in the archonship of Pythodorus [404/3]. Having become masters of the city, they ignored the other resolutions about the constitution, but appointed five hundred councillors and the other officials from a short list of a thousand, and to support themselves chose ten governors of the Piraeus, eleven guardians of the gaol and three hundred attendants armed with whips; thus they gained control of the city. (2) At first they were moderate towards the citizens, and pretended that their aim was the traditional constitution. They took down from the Areopagus hill the laws of Ephialtes and Archestratus about the council of the Areopagus; and they annulled the laws of Solon which provided scope for disagreement, and the discretionary power which was left to jurors, in order to amend the constitution and leave no opportunity for disagreement. For instance, in the matter of a man's bequeathing his property to whoever he likes, the Thirty gave the testator full and absolute power, and removed the attached difficulties ('except when he is insane or senile, or under the influence of a woman'), so that there should be no way in for malicious prosecutors; and they did likewise in the other cases. (3) That is how they behaved at first. They eliminated malicious prosecutors, and those who curried favour with the people contrary to what was best and were harmful and wicked; and the city was pleased with these achievements, thinking that the Thirty were acting from good motives. (4) But when they had a firmer hold on the city they left none of the citizens alone, but put to death those who were outstanding for their wealth, birth or reputation, cunningly removing those whom they had cause to fear and whose property they wanted to plunder. Within a short space of time they had killed no fewer than fifteen hundred.

36

(1) When the city was declining in this way, Theramenes, annoyed at what was happening, urged the Thirty to abandon their outrageous behaviour and give the best men a share in affairs. At first they opposed him; but when his arguments gained currency among the masses and the ordinary people became well disposed to him, they grew afraid that he might become champion of the people and overthrow the ruling clique. They therefore began to draw up a register of three thousand of the citizens, as if to give them a share in the control of the state. (2) Theramenes objected again to this, first because they wanted to give a share to the better sort, but were going to give a share only to three thousand, as if good qualities were limited to that number; and secondly because they were trying to do two completely incompatible things: set up a regime based on force, and make the rulers weaker than the subjects. But they took no notice of these complaints. For a long time they postponed publishing the register of the Three Thousand, and kept to themselves the names of those whom they had decided on, and whenever they did think they might publish it they deleted some of the men who had been included and included in their place some who had been left out.

37

(1) When it was already winter, Thrasybulus and the exiles occupied Phyle. When the Thirty had failed with the force which they led out against him, they decided to disarm the unprivileged and to destroy Theramenes in the following way. They introduced two laws and ordered the council to approve them: one giving the Thirty full authority to put to death those citizens who were not included in the register of the Three Thousand; the other excluding from participation in the present constitution whoever had helped to demolish the fortification at Eetionea, or had taken any action against the Four Hundred who had set up the previous oligarchy. Theramenes had been involved in both of these things, so when the laws were ratified the result was that he was excluded from the citizen body and the Thirty had the power to put him to death.

(2) After eliminating Theramenes they disarmed all except the Three Thousand, and in other respects they turned to savagery and wickedness on a large scale. They sent envoys to Sparta, to make accusations against Theramenes and to ask for help. The Spartans responded by sending Callibius as garrison commander with about seven hundred soldiers, and these on their arrival garrisoned the Acropolis.

38

(1) Next the men from Phyle occupied Munichia, and defeated in battle those who came to attack them with the Thirty. After this clash the men from the city withdrew. The next day they assembled in the Agora, deposed the Thirty, and elected ten of the citizens with full authority to put an end to the war. However, these men on taking office did not do what they were appointed to do, but sent to Sparta to ask for help and borrow money. (2) Those who belonged to the citizen body were annoyed at this: afraid that their power would be overthrown, and wanting to inspire fear in the others (which they succeeded in doing), they arrested and put to death Demaretus, who was second to none of the citizens; and they took a firm grip on affairs with the support of Callibius, the Peloponnesians who were present, and also some of the cavalry. (The cavalry included some of the citizens most anxious to prevent the return of the men from Phyle.) (3) When the whole of the people went over to the men occupying the Piraeus and Munichia, and these were getting the upper hand in the war, the men in the city deposed the first board of Ten and appointed another Ten, those who seemed to be the best men: under these Ten, and with their enthusiastic support, the reconciliation took place and the people returned to Athens. Chief among them were Rhinon of Paeania and Phayllus of Acherdus: before Pausanias's arrival they sent messages to the men at the Piraeus, and after he had come they joined eagerly in working for the return. (4) The peace settlement and reconciliation were brought to a conclusion by Pausanias, king of Sparta, together with the ten peace commissioners who subsequently came from Sparta at his urgent request. Rhinon and his supporters were praised for their good will towards the people: having accepted responsibility

under the oligarchy they submitted to examination under the democracy, and no complaint was made against them either by those who had remained in the city or by those who had returned from the Piraeus; indeed, on account of this Rhinon was immediately elected general.

39

(1) The reconciliation took place in the archonship of Euclides [403/2], in accordance with the following agreements. Of the Athenians who had remained in the city, those who wished to emigrate might occupy Eleusis, retain their rights as citizens, with full power and authority over themselves, and continue to draw the revenues from their own property. (2) The sanctuary at Eleusis was to be common to both communities, under the care of the Heralds and Eumolpidae in accordance with tradition. No one from Eleusis was to go to the city, and no one from the city was to go to Eleusis, except in each case for the Mysteries. Those at Eleusis were to contribute to the alliance from their revenues in the same way as the rest of the Athenians. (3) If anyone who emigrated took a house at Eleusis, he was to seek agreement with the owner; if they were unable to agree, each should choose three assessors, and the owner should accept whatever price they fixed. Any of the people of Eleusis might join in the community if they were approved by the new settlers. (4) Those who wished to emigrate to Eleusis should be entitled to register, in the case of those already in the city of Athens, within ten days of swearing the oaths to the reconciliation, and to emigrate within twenty days; in the case of those who were away from Athens, within the same period from their return. (5) No one living at Eleusis should be entitled to hold any office in the city, without cancelling his registration and returning to live in the city. Trials for homicide should be held in accordance with tradition in cases where a man had himself performed the act of killing or wounding. (6) Otherwise no one was to recall the past misdeeds of anyone except the Thirty, the Ten, the Eleven and the governors of the Piraeus, and not even of these if they successfully submitted to an examination. The examination was to take place, for the governors of the Piraeus, among the men of the Piraeus; for those

who had held office in the city, among those possessed of a property qualification. Alternatively, those who were not willing to submit to an examination might emigrate. Each side was to repay separately the money that it had borrowed for the war.

40

(1) Those were the terms on which the reconciliation took place. The men who had fought on the side of the Thirty were afraid, and many intended to emigrate but postponed their registration until the last possible days, as everyone is apt to do. But Archinus, since he saw how many they were and wanted to keep them back, took away the remaining days for registration, so that many were compelled to remain, unwillingly, until their confidence returned. (2) It seems that Archinus's policy was good both in this matter and, afterwards, when he attacked in a prosecution for illegal proposal the motion of Thrasybulus which was to give a share in the citizenship to all who had joined in the return from the Piraeus, some of whom were palpably slaves. There was a third instance, when someone who had returned began to ignore the amnesty, and Archinus haled him before the council and persuaded it to have him put to death without a regular trial, saying that now was the time to show whether they were willing to preserve the democracy and abide by their oaths: if they let this man go they would allow the others to behave in the same way, but if they executed him they would set an example to all. That is what happened: when this man had been put to death, no one afterwards ever broke the amnesty. (3) On this occasion, it seems, the Athenians reacted to their previous misfortunes, both individually and together, better and more public-spiritedly than anyone else at any other time. Not only did they wipe out all prosecutions for past acts, but, since it was thought that this should be the first step in establishing concord, the state repaid to Sparta the money which the Thirty had received for the war, although the agreements stipulated that those from the city and those from the Piraeus were to repay their debts separately. When democracies come to power in other cities, however, far from making voluntary payments out of their own property, the democrats redistribute the land. (4) The Athenians were

reconciled with the men who had settled at Eleusis in the third year after their emigration, the archonship of Xenaenetus [401/0].

41

(1) That final reconciliation took place subsequently. Meanwhile the people gained control of affairs and set up the present constitution, in the archonship of Pythodorus [404/3]: the people's taking political power seems justifiable, since it was the people themselves who achieved their return.

K CONCLUSION TO FIRST PART (Chapter 41.2–3)

The Athenian Constitution's *historical survey ends at the end of the fifth century: although the work was written some seventy years later, and there had been several piecemeal modifications during those seventy years, there had been no abrupt change which could be represented as a further change in the constitution. Mistakenly, our author believed that the effect of the piecemeal adjustments since 403 had been to make the democracy ever more extreme. To summarize his history he provides a list of (originally) eleven constitutional changes by which Athens developed from the primitive monarchy to the democracy of the fourth century, some of them moves towards democracy (each of these taking Athens further than the previous such move) and others moves away from it. The list is the author's own summary of the preceding narrative: it corresponds to that narrative as the list of aristocratic and democratic leaders in chapter 28 does not. A reference to Draco was added when the 'Constitution of Draco' was added in chapter 4, and this disrupts the original numbered sequence.*

41

(2) This was the eleventh of the changes in the constitution. The first modification of the original arrangements occurred when Ion and the people with him came as settlers: that is when the Athenians were first divided into the four tribes and the tribal heads

were instituted. Second, and first after this, involving a form of constitution, the change under Theseus, which deviated slightly from monarchy. Next, that under Draco, in which laws were written out for the first time. Third, that under Solon after the civil disturbances, the change which brought about the origin of the democracy. Fourth, the tyranny of Pisistratus. Fifth, the constitution of Cleisthenes after the overthrow of the tyrants, more democratic than Solon's constitution. Sixth, the constitution after the Persian Wars, when the council of the Areopagus took charge. Seventh and next, the constitution to which Aristides pointed and which Ephialtes accomplished by overthrowing the council of the Areopagus: in this the city made its greatest mistakes, because of the demagogues and its rule of the sea. Eighth, the establishment of the Four Hundred; and after that, ninth, democracy again. Tenth, the tyranny of the Thirty and the Ten. Eleventh, the regime after the return from Phyle and the Piraeus, from which the constitution has continued to that in force today, continually increasing the power of the masses. The people have made themselves masters of everything, and control all things by means of decrees and jury-courts, in which the sovereign power resides with the people; even the jurisdiction of the council has been transferred to the people. The Athenians seem to be right to follow this line, for it is easier to corrupt the few than the many, whether by money or by favours. (3) At first they decided not to pay stipends for attendance at the assembly. But when men were staying away from the assembly, and the *prytanes* were trying various devices to bring the masses in to ratify the voting, first Agyrrhius provided for the payment of one obol, after him Heraclides of Clazomenae, the man known as 'king', raised it to two obols, and then Agyrrhius again raised it to three obols.

L   REGISTRATION AND TRAINING OF CITIZENS (Chapter 42)

After summarizing the history of the constitution, our author embarks on an analysis of the constitution in his own day. Chapter 42 is devoted to the registration and training of the citizens at their coming of age, chapters 43–62 to public officials, and chapters 63–9 to the jury-courts: the source of our author's information, and probably of his arrangement of the material, is the Athenian code of laws, revised and systematized at the end of the fifth century.

Chapter 42 begins with the scrutiny and registration of citizens at the new year after their eighteenth birthday: probably not only Athenian parentage on both sides but also legitimate birth was required, although this is not stated in the text, and probably both the criterion of freedom and that of age could be considered both by the court and by the council. The latter part of the chapter is devoted to a compulsory two-year period of cadet training which followed registration. Our author does not here contrast current with earlier practice, as he is to do at several later points, but other evidence makes it clear that this compulsory programme was instituted about 335/4, as one of the measures taken to restore Athens' morale and military strength after her defeat by Philip of Macedon at Chaeronea in 338. The scrutiny of young citizens is attested at the end of the fifth century, and the oath sworn by the cadets appears to be an ancient oath. Before 335/4 cadets already existed as a separate category of citizens, and could perform guard duties; then the compulsory programme was introduced; towards the end of the fourth century service was reduced to one year and ceased to be compulsory. Our author implies that the compulsory service was for all citizens, and in chapter 53 he implies that all citizens were required to serve as arbitrators in their forty-second year on the registers; but the cadets' training was hoplite training, and probably both the unfit and the members of the lowest of Solon's four classes (chapter 7) were exempt.

42

(1) The present form of the constitution is as follows. Men belong to the citizen body if they are of citizen parentage on both sides, and they are registered as members of their demes at the age of eighteen. When they are registered, the deme members take a vote about them on oath, first to decide whether they have reached the age prescribed by the law (if they decide that they have not, the candidates return to the ranks of the boys), and secondly to decide whether they are free men and born as prescribed by the laws. Then, if they reject a man as unfree, he appeals to the jury-court, and

the deme members choose five of their own number as prosecutors: if he is found to have been unjustly registered, the state sells him as a slave; if he wins the case, the deme members are obliged to register him. (2) After this the council scrutinizes those who have been registered, and if anyone is found to be below the age of eighteen it punishes the deme members who have registered him. When the cadets have been scrutinized, their fathers meet by tribes and choose on oath three members of the tribe over forty years old whom they consider the best and most suitable to take charge of the cadets: from these the people elect one man from each tribe as *sophronistes*, and from the citizen body as a whole they elect a single *cosmetes* as supreme commander of the whole force. (3) The cadets assemble under these officers, and first make a tour of the sanctuaries, then proceed to the Piraeus, where some do guard duty at Munichia and some at Acte. The people also elect two trainers for them, and instructors to teach them infantry fighting, archery, javelin-throwing and catapult-firing. For maintenance one drachma each is provided for the *sophronistae* and four obols for the cadets: each *sophronistes* takes the funds of his tribe members, buys a common stock of provisions for all of them (for they eat by tribes), and takes charge of everything else. (4) That is how the first year is spent. The following year there is an assembly in the theatre, at which the cadets display to the people the manoeuvres which they have learned and receive a shield and a spear from the state. Then they patrol the frontiers of the country, and spend their time in the guard-posts. (5) These two years they spend on guard duty, wearing short cloaks. They are free from all obligations; and so that they shall have no reason for absence they are not allowed to appear in lawsuits either as prosecutor or as defendant, except in cases concerning an inheritance or an heiress. Absence is allowed if a man holds a hereditary priesthood. At the end of the two years the cadets join the rest of the citizen body.

M OFFICIALS, APPOINTED BY LOT AND BY ELECTION: THE COUNCIL (Chapters 43–9)

The longest section of the second part of the Athenian Constitution *is devoted to a survey of public officials, within which there are major sub-sections on the council (43.2–49) and the nine archons (55–9). 43.1 consists of an introductory note dividing officials into those appointed by lot and those appointed by election. Most civilian offices were felt to require loyalty rather than skill, and allotment was used as an appropriate method for distributing appointments fairly among men considered equally eligible; military offices required ability and the confidence of the men serving under the officers, and so these were filled by election. When our author turns in chapter 61 to elected officials he deals with the military officers only, and the elected civilian officials are forgotten.*

Discussion of the council begins with its organization (43.2–44): what is said about meetings both of the council and of the assembly is fitted in here; there is no separate treatment of the assembly, and no mention at all of the separate body of legislators (nomothetae) which in the fourth century enacted 'laws' as opposed to 'decrees'. The following chapters are devoted to the various powers of the council: limitations on its jurisdiction (45.1–3); preparation of business for the assembly (45.4); its duties in connection with the navy (46.1), and with public works (46.2); its supervision of financial officials (47–8); and the scrutinies which it conducts (49).

43

(1) That is what happens with the registration of the citizens, and with the cadets. All the officials concerned with civilian administration are appointed by lot, apart from the treasurer of the army fund, the men in charge of the festival fund and the curator of the water supply: these are elected, and hold office from one Panathenaea to the next. All the military officers are elected also.

(2) There is a council of five hundred appointed by lot, fifty members from each tribe. Each tribe's members in turn, as determined by lot, form the prytany, the first four for thirty-six days each and the remaining six for thirty-five days each (the year is a

lunar year). (3) First the members of the prytany eat together in the Round House, at the state's expense. Then they convene meetings both of the council and of the people: the council every day, except when there is a day of exemption, the people four times in each prytany. They prescribe what business the council is to deal with, what business on each particular day, and where it is to meet. (4) Likewise they prescribe the meetings of the assembly. One in each prytany is the Principal Assembly, at which there is a vote of confidence to decide whether the officials are doing their duty satisfactorily, and the food supply and the defence of the country are discussed. On these occasions anyone who wishes may make a denunciation; and lists of confiscated property, and claims to inheritances and to heiresses, are read out, so that nothing shall escape anyone's notice and go unclaimed. (5) In the sixth prytany, in addition to the business mentioned above, the *prytanes* take a vote as to whether an ostracism should be held or not; and they invite complaints against malicious prosecutors, three against Athenians and three against metics, and complaints against anyone who has made a promise to the people and failed to keep it. (6) The second assembly of the prytany is devoted to supplications: anyone who wishes may supplicate on whatever matter he wishes, private or public, and address the people. The remaining two are devoted to other business, and for them the laws prescribe that three religious matters should be dealt with, three concerning heralds and embassies, and three secular. Sometimes business is taken without a preliminary vote. Heralds and envoys go to the *prytanes* first, and bearers of letters deliver them to the *prytanes*.

44

(1) There is a single chairman of the *prytanes*, appointed by lot: he is in charge for a night and a day, and the same man is not allowed to serve longer than that or on a second occasion. This man keeps the keys of the sanctuaries in which the state's funds and records are stored, and the public seal, and he and a third of the *prytanes* designated by him are obliged to remain on duty in the Round House. (2) Whenever the *prytanes* convene a meeting of the council or the people, this man picks by lot a presiding

committee of nine, one councillor from each tribe except the tribe in prytany, and again picks one of the nine to be chairman, and he hands the list of agenda to them. (3) They take over the agenda, are responsible for good order, put forward the subjects to be dealt with, determine the results of the voting, are in charge of all other arrangements and have the power to close the meeting. A man may not be chairman more than once in the year, but may serve on the committee once in each prytany. (4) The election of generals, cavalry commanders and the other military officers is held in the assembly, in whatever way the people see fit: this election is held by the first prytany after the sixth in whose term of office there are good omens. A preliminary resolution of the council is necessary for this business too.

45

(1) Formerly the council had full power to impose fines, to imprison and to put to death. When it had taken Lysimachus to the executioner, and he was sitting waiting for the death sentence to be carried out, Eumelides of Alopece took him away, saying that no citizen ought to be put to death except by the sentence of a jury-court. A trial was held in court: Lysimachus was acquitted, and came to be known as the man who returned from the garotte. The people then took away from the council the right to execute, imprison and fine, and enacted a law that, if the council convicted a man of wrongdoing or wanted to punish him, its convictions and punishments should be brought before the jury-court by the *thesmothetae*, and whatever the jurors voted should be final. (2) The council has jurisdiction over most officials, especially those who handle money: its judgement is not final but referrable to the jury-court. It is possible also for private citizens to make a denunciation against any official whom they wish, on a charge of not complying with the laws: here too there is reference to the jury-court if the council convicts. (3) The council holds a scrutiny of those who are to serve in the council for the following year and of the nine archons. Formerly it had final power to reject any of them, but now there is reference to the jury-court in these cases. (4) In those matters the council does not have final power. It presents preliminary resolutions to the people,

and the people are not permitted to decide anything which is not the subject of a preliminary resolution and placed on the agenda by the *prytanes*: on this count the man who carried the motion is liable to a prosecution for illegal proposal.

46

(1) The council is responsible for the triremes that have already been built, and for the equipment and the ship-sheds; and it has new triremes or quadriremes built, whichever the people decide, and equipment and ship-sheds for them. The people elect designers for the ships. If the council does not hand over this work complete to the next year's council, it is not entitled to receive its award (the award is made under the next year's council). It sees to the building of the triremes by electing ten of its own members as trireme-builders. (2) Also the council inspects all public buildings; and if it judges anyone guilty it reports him to the people, convicts him and hands him over to a jury-court.

47

(1) In general the council cooperates in the administrative work of the other officials. First there are ten treasurers of Athena, one appointed by lot from each tribe, from the five-hundred-bushel class in accordance with Solon's law (this law is still in force): the men who are appointed hold office even if they are quite poor. These take over from their predecessors the statue of Athena, the Victories, the other equipment and the money, in the presence of the council. (2) Next there are ten sellers, one appointed by lot from each tribe. They are responsible for all leases, and let out the contracts for the mines and the taxes, in conjunction with the treasurer of the army fund and the men elected to take charge of the festival fund, in the presence of the council; they ratify the award, to whoever the council makes it, of the leases for active mines, which are let for three years, and for abandoned mines, which are let for seven years. They sell the confiscated property of men who have gone into exile after a trial before the Areopagus and of other convicted men, and the sale is ratified by the nine archons. In the case of taxes leased

for the year they write on whitewashed tablets the name of the lessee and the price of the lease, and hand these over to the council. (3) They keep separate records of those who have to make a payment every prytany, with ten tablets for each, those who have to make a payment three times in the year, with a tablet for each payment, and those who have to pay in the ninth prytany of the year. They keep records also of the lands and the houses which have been inventoried and ordered to be sold by the jury-court (the sellers sell these too). The price of houses has to be paid in five years, and the price of land in ten: these payments are made in the ninth prytany. (4) The *basileus* introduces the leases of sacred lands, recording them on whitewashed tablets. These too are let for ten years, and the payment is made in the ninth prytany: so most of the money is collected in this prytany. (5) The tablets, written out according to the times of payment, are brought in to the council and kept by the public slave. When there is a payment of money he hands these same tablets to the receivers, taking down from the racks those relating to the men who have to pay money and have their records deleted on the day in question. The other tablets are kept separately so that they shall not be deleted prematurely.

48

(1) There are ten receivers, appointed tribally by lot: they take over the tablets and delete the sums paid, in the presence of the council in the council-house, and give back the tablets to the public slave again. If anyone misses his payment, he is recorded there, and is obliged to pay double the missing sum or go to prison: the council has full power to exact these sums and to imprison in accordance with the laws. (2) On the first day the receivers receive all the payments and allocate them to the officials. On the next day they introduce the allocation: they write it on a tablet, read it out in the council-house, and put it forward for debate in the council, in case anyone is aware that any official or private individual has committed an offence with regard to the allocation. If it does appear that anyone has committed an offence, proposals are put to the vote. (3) The councillors appoint by lot ten auditors from their own number to check the officials' accounts each prytany. (4) They also

appoint examiners by lot, one from each tribe, and two assistants for each of the examiners. These men are obliged to sit in market hours by the statue of the hero of each tribe: if anyone wishes to make any charge, private or public, against an official who has presented his accounts in the jury-court, within thirty days of his doing so, he writes on a whitewashed tablet his own name, the defendant's name and the offence of which he accuses him, adds whatever assessment he thinks right, and gives it to the examiner. (5) The examiner takes it and reads it, and if he decides there is a case to answer he hands private accusations to the deme justices who give verdicts for the tribe in question, and reports public accusations to the *thesmothetae*. The *thesmothetae*, when they receive an accusation, introduce this examination into the jury-court again, and whatever the jurors decide has final validity.

49

(1) The council holds a scrutiny of the cavalry's horses, and if it finds that any man has a good horse but is not maintaining it well it punishes him by withholding the fodder grant. Horses which are unable to keep up, or are unwilling to stay in line and are unmanageable, it brands on the jaw with the sign of a wheel, and any horse which has been branded is rejected. It also holds a scrutiny of the *prodromi*, to see which men appear capable of serving, and if it rejects anyone his service is at an end. Likewise it holds a scrutiny of the *hamippi*, and if it rejects anyone that is the end of his paid service. (2) The cavalrymen are registered by the registrars, ten men elected by the people: they give the names of the men whom they propose to register to the cavalry commanders and squadron commanders. These officers take over the register and bring it in to the council. They then open the sealed tablet containing the names of those who are currently cavalrymen, delete any men already listed who declare on oath that they are physically incapable of serving, and call up those newly registered. If any of the latter declares on oath that he is physically or financially unable to serve, they let him go; if not, the councillors vote as to whether or not he is fit to serve in the cavalry; if they elect him, they enter him on the tablet, but if not, they let him go too. (3) The council used to judge the

plans for the robe; but this is now done by a jury-court picked by lot, for the councillors appeared to be giving their decision as a favour. The council shares with the treasurer of the army fund the responsibility for the making of Victories, and for prizes for the Panathenaea. (4) The council also scrutinizes the invalids: there is a law which prescribes that men who possess less than three minas and are so maimed in their bodies that they cannot do any work are to be scrutinized by the council and given a public maintenance grant of two obols a day each. The councillors have a treasurer appointed by lot. (5) In general, one might say, the council cooperates in the administrative work of the other officials.

N OFFICIALS APPOINTED ANNUALLY BY LOT
(Chapters 50–54)

Between the council and the nine archons our author includes in his survey of officials appointed annually by lot a catalogue of miscellaneous officials. He begins with those concerned with city facilities (50–51); then passes to those concerned with the administration of justice (52–3). In the course of chapter 53 he is led from the Forty to the public arbitrators (who served for a year but were not appointed by lot), and from the use of the forty-two year-classes in the appointment of the arbitrators to the use of the year-classes in the army. In chapter 54 he returns to annual officials. He mentions first the roadbuilders (section 1), who might have been mentioned in 50–51; then the annual auditors (section 2), whom he treats separately from the examining officials of 48.3–5 because those were members of the council but these were not; then three secretaries (sections 3–5), the last of whom was believed to require special skill and was therefore elected; then two boards of religious officials called hieropoei (sections 6–7); and finally he is led from the hieropoei to two other officials whose duties included the organization of festivals (section 8).

At any rate with the secretaries and the hieropoei, our author has been selective: altogether six state secretaries are found in contemporary documents, and there were several boards of hieropoei. On the other hand, the detailed account of the forty-two year-classes

*is not necessary here: probably the Athenians were proud of this
elaborate scheme, as they were proud of the elaborate scheme by
which they sought to secure fairness in the running of the jury-
courts (63–9), and the* Athenian Constitution's *detailed treatment
reflects this pride.*

50

(1) That is the work handled by the council. There are appointed
by lot repairers of temples, a board of ten men, who are given thirty
minas by the receivers and repair the temples which are most in
need of attention. (2) Also there are ten city magistrates, of whom
five hold office in the Piraeus and five in the city. These see that
the girls who play the pipes, the harp and the lyre are not hired
for more than two drachmae, and if several men are eager to secure
the same girl they draw lots and hire her out to the winner. They
see that none of the dung-collectors deposits dung within ten stades
of the city wall. They prevent buildings which encroach on the
streets, balconies which extend over the streets, overhead drainpipes
which discharge into the street, and window-shutters which open
into the street. Using public slaves for the purpose, they remove
for burial the bodies of those who die in the streets.

51

(1) Likewise there are appointed by lot ten market magistrates, five
for the Piraeus and five for the city. These are required by the laws
to take responsibility for all goods that are on sale, to ensure that
what is sold is in good condition and genuine. (2) Also ten measures
magistrates are appointed by lot, five for the city and five for the
Piraeus. They are responsible for all measures and weights, to ensure
that the salesmen use honest standards. (3) There used to be ten
corn-guardians appointed by lot, five for the Piraeus and five for
the city, but now there are twenty for the city and fifteen for the
Piraeus. They are responsible for seeing, first, that the unground
corn is sold honestly in the market, and then that the millers sell
the meal in accordance with the price which they paid for the barley-
corn, and that the bread-sellers sell the loaves in accordance with

the price which they paid for the wheat and that their loaves are of the prescribed weight (the law requires these magistrates to prescribe the weight of loaves). (4) Ten overseers of the exchange are appointed by lot: they are bidden to take responsibility for the exchanges, and to compel the dealers to convey to the city two thirds of the corn which is brought into the corn market.

52

(1) The Eleven are appointed by lot. Their task is to take charge of men in the gaol. When thieves, kidnappers and highwaymen are delivered before them, if they admit their guilt, the Eleven put them to death; if they dispute the charge, they bring them before the jury-court: then, if they are acquitted, they let them go, and if not, they put them to death. When land and houses are registered for confiscation, the Eleven bring these before the jury-court, and those which are judged to be forfeit to the state they hand over to the sellers. They also bring indications before the court: these are among the cases introduced by the Eleven, but some of the indications are introduced by the *thesmothetae*. (2) Five men are appointed by lot as introducers, to introduce the monthly suits, each man acting for two tribes. The monthly suits are: for a dowry, when a man owes a dowry and fails to hand it over; if a man borrows at a rate of 1 per cent per month and defaults; if a man wishes to ply his trade in the Agora, borrows capital from someone and defaults; also suits for battery; suits concerning friendly loans; concerning associations; for slaves and yoke-animals; concerning trierarchies; and concerning banking. (3) The introducers are responsible for these, and introduce them as monthly suits. Likewise the receivers handle suits initiated by and suits against tax-collectors: in matters up to ten drachmae they have the final right of decision, the others they introduce to the jury-court as monthly suits.

53

(1) The Forty, four appointed by lot from each tribe, are the officials from whom plaintiffs obtain a hearing in the other private suits. Earlier they were thirty in number, and used to go round the

demes trying cases, but since the oligarchy of the Thirty there have been forty of them. (2) Cases up to ten drachmae they have absolute authority to decide, cases above this assessment they hand over to the arbitrators. The arbitrators take the cases over, and if they are unable to bring about a settlement they give a verdict. If both parties are satisfied with the verdict and abide by it, the case is at an end. If either of the litigants appeals to the jury-court, the litigants place the testimonies, challenges and laws in jars, those of the plaintiff and those of the defendant separately; the jars are sealed, with the verdict of the arbitrator, written on a tablet, fastened to them, and handed over to the four members of the Forty who act for the tribe of the defendant. (3) These men take over the case and introduce it into the jury-court, those up to 1,000 drachmae into a court of two hundred and one, and those over 1,000 drachmae into a court of four hundred and one; no laws, challenges or testimonies may be used except those which were cited before the arbitrator and placed in the jars. (4) The arbitrators are men in their sixtieth year: this is clear from the archons and the eponymous heroes (there are ten heroes of the tribes, and forty-two heroes of the year-classes). The cadets on their enrolment used to be listed on whitewashed tablets, together with the name of the archon in whose year they were enrolled and the hero of the year-class which had provided the arbitrators of the previous year; now they are inscribed on a bronze pillar, and the pillar is set up in front of the council-house, near the statues of the tribal heroes. (5) The Forty take as arbitrators the men in the last year-class, assign their tribal responsibilities to them, and draw lots for the cases which each is to take: it is obligatory for each man to complete the arbitration of the cases which fall to him. The law prescribes that if a man refuses to serve as arbitrator when his age has come he is to be deprived of his civic rights, unless he is holding office that year or is away from Athens: only those men are exempt. (6) If any litigant is wronged by the arbitrator, it is open to him to make a denunciation to the board of arbitrators, and if they convict, the laws prescribe that the offender is to be deprived of his civic rights. Here too there is a right of appeal to the jury-court. (7) The forty-two heroes are used for military campaigns also: when an age-group is sent out, it is announced that those from a certain archon and a certain hero to a certain other archon and a certain other hero are required to serve.

54

(1) The following officials are appointed by lot also. Five road-builders, who have public slaves to work for them and whose duty is to repair the roads. (2) Also ten auditors, and ten advocates for them, with whom all men who have held office are required to deposit their accounts. These are the men who check the accounts of those subject to examination, and who introduce the examination into the jury-court. If they prove that a man is an embezzler, the jurors convict him of embezzlement and the sum determined is repaid tenfold; if they prove that a man has taken bribes and the jurors convict him, an assessment for bribery is made and this sum also is repaid tenfold; if a man is convicted of misdemeanour, an assessment for misdemeanour is made, and here the simple amount is repaid if a man discharges the debt before the ninth prytany of the year, or if he fails to do that it is doubled. Tenfold payments are not doubled. (3) The secretary called the prytany secretary is appointed by lot: he is in charge of documents, keeps the texts of decrees that are enacted, checks all other records and attends meetings of the council. Previously this was an elected office, and the most distinguished and the most trusted men were elected to it (for on the pillars on which texts were inscribed this secretary is named in connection with alliances, appointments of *proxeni* and grants of citizenship); but now it is filled by lot. (4) Another secretary is appointed by lot, the one in charge of laws: he attends meetings of the council and checks the recording of all laws. (5) The assembly elects a secretary to read documents to itself and to the council, and he has no responsibility other than reading. (6) Ten *hieropoei* are appointed by lot, those entitled the *hieropoei* in charge of expiatory sacrifices, who make the sacrifices ordered by oracles and when necessary cooperate with the soothsayers to seek good omens. (7) There are another ten appointed by lot, entitled the annual *hieropoei*, who perform certain sacrifices and administer all the quadrennial festivals except the Panathenaea. The quadrennial

festivals are: first the pilgrimage to Delos (there is also a sexennial festival there), secondly the Brauronia, thirdly the Heraclea, fourthly the Eleusinia, fifthly the Panathenaea. None of the four occurs in the same year. Now, in the archonship of Cephisophon [329/8], the Hephaestia has been added. (8) A governor for Salamis and a demarch for the Piraeus are appointed by lot also: these hold the Dionysia in each place and appoint the *choregi*. In Salamis the name of the governor is published.

O THE NINE ARCHONS (Chapters 55–9)

The survey of officials appointed annually by lot concludes with the nine archons. Our author begins with their appointment and scrutiny (55–56.1), reviews in turn the religious and the judicial duties of the archon (56.2–7), the basileus *(57), the polemarch (58) and (judicial duties only) the* thesmothetae *(59.1–6), and ends with a duty shared by the whole college, the allocation of jurors to courts (59.7, treated in more detail in 63–5).*

55

(1) Those officials are appointed by lot, and are responsible for all the matters mentioned. As for the so-called nine archons, the manner of their appointment from the beginning has been stated above; now six *thesmothetae* and their secretary, the archon, the *basileus* and the polemarch are appointed by lot from each tribe in turn. (2) They are scrutinized first in the council of five hundred (apart from the secretary, who is scrutinized in a jury-court only, like the other officials: all officials appointed by lot or by election have to undergo a scrutiny before entering office), the nine archons being scrutinized in the council and again in a jury-court. Previously, no one whom the council rejected could hold office, but now there is reference to the jury-court, and the court has the final right of decision in the scrutiny. (3) When the archons are scrutinized, they are asked first, 'Who is your father, and from which deme? Who is your father's father? Who is your mother? Who is your mother's father, and from which deme?' Then the archons are asked whether they have a cult

of Apollo of Ancestry and Zeus of the Courtyard, and where the sanctuaries of these are; whether they have family tombs, and where these are; whether they treat their parents well; whether they pay their taxes; whether they have performed their military service. After asking these questions, the presiding magistrate says, 'Call witnesses to these things.' (4) When witnesses have been produced, he asks, 'Does anyone wish to accuse this man?' If there is an accuser, the magistrate allows accusation and reply, and then puts the question to the vote, by show of hands in the council, by ballot in the court. If there is no accuser, he puts it to the vote immediately: in these cases, previously, one man would cast a token vote, but now it is obligatory for all the jurors to vote on the candidates, so that, if a crooked man has disposed of his accusers, it will be possible for the jurors to reject him. (5) After undergoing this scrutiny, the archons proceed to the stone, on which the sliced victims have been placed (on this same stone the arbitrators take an oath before giving their arbitration, and witnesses swear when denying evidence attributed to them). They climb on to the stone, and swear that they will exercise their office justly and in accordance with the laws, and will not take bribes on account of their office or, if they do so, will dedicate a golden statue. After taking the oath they proceed from there to the Acropolis, and take the same oath again there. They then enter on their office.

56

(1) The archon, the *basileus* and the polemarch each have two assistants, men of their own choice: these men are scrutinized in the jury-court before entering office, and submit to an examination after leaving office.

(2) The archon, as soon as he has entered on his office, first makes a proclamation, that whatever each man possessed before his entry into office he shall possess and control until the end of it. (3) Next he appoints *choregi* for the tragedies, the three richest men of all the Athenians; formerly he also appointed five *choregi* for the comedies, but these are now supplied by the tribes. The tribes supply *choregi* for the Dionysia (for men's choruses, boys' choruses and comedies) and for the Thargelia (for men's choruses and boys'

choruses): for choruses at the Dionysia *choregi* are appointed by individual tribes, for those at the Thargelia one is appointed for two tribes and the individual tribes supply them in turn. The archon receives the names of the tribally appointed *choregi*. Then he holds challenges to an exchange, and introduces into court claims for exemption, when a man claims that he has performed this liturgy before, or is exempt because he has performed another liturgy and his period of exemption is not yet over, or has not reached the required age (*choregi* for boys' choruses must be over forty years old). He also appoints *choregi* for Delos, and a pilgrimage-leader for the thirty-oared ship which takes the young men. (4) He is responsible for processions: that for Asclepius, when the initiates stay indoors; and that at the Great Dionysia, in conjunction with the overseers. There are ten overseers of the Dionysia: formerly they were elected by the people and bore the expenses of the procession themselves, but now one is appointed by lot from each tribe and they are given one hundred minas for their equipment. (5) The archon is responsible also for the procession at the Thargelia and the procession for Zeus the Saviour. Those are the festivals for which he is responsible. (6) The following public and private lawsuits fall to him, and he holds the preliminary inquiry and introduces them into the jury-court: maltreatment of parents (on this charge anyone who wishes may prosecute without risk of penalty); maltreatment of orphans (where the suit is against the guardians); maltreatment of an heiress (where the suit is against the guardians or the husband); maltreatment of an orphan's estate (against the guardians again); insanity, when a man is accused of squandering his property through insanity; for the appointment of distributors, if anyone objects to the administration of property in common; for the appointment of a guardian; for the adjudication of a guardianship; for displaying to public view; for having oneself appointed guardian; adjudications of estates and of heiresses. (7) He has the oversight of orphans, heiresses and women who at the death of their husband claim to be pregnant; and he has full power to impose a summary fine on the offenders or to bring them before the jury-court. He lets out the estates of orphans, and of heiresses until they reach the age of fourteen, and receives the valuations of the security offered by the lessees; and if guardians do not give the children their maintenance he exacts it.

57

(1) Those are the responsibilities of the archon. The *basileus* is first responsible for the Mysteries, in conjunction with the overseers elected by the people (two from all Athenians, one from the Eumolpidae, one from the Heralds). Next for the Dionysia at the Lenaeum: this involves a procession and a contest; the procession is the joint responsibility of the *basileus* and the overseers, the contest is organized by the *basileus*. He also organizes all the torch-races; and one might say that he administers all the traditional sacrifices. (2) Public lawsuits fall to him on charges of impiety, and when a man is involved in a dispute with someone else over a priesthood. He holds the adjudications for clans and for priests in all their disputes on religious matters. Also all private suits for homicide fall to him, and it is he who makes the proclamation that the killer is excluded from the things specified by law. (3) The following are the suits for homicide and wounding. Trials are held at the Areopagus, when anyone intentionally kills or wounds; for poisoning, when anyone kills by this means; and for arson: these are the only charges tried by the council of the Areopagus. For unintentional homicide, for planning homicide, and for killing a slave, metic or foreigner, the court at the Palladium is used. When someone admits to killing, but claims to have done so in accordance with the laws (for instance, if he has caught an adulterer, killed in ignorance in war, or killed as a competitor in the games), the trial is held at the Delphinium. If anyone is accused of killing or wounding somebody while in exile on a charge for which reconciliation is possible, the trial is held at the sanctuary of Phreatus; (4) the accused makes his defence from a boat moored offshore. Apart from the cases tried by the Areopagus, these are tried by fifty-one men appointed by lot; the *basileus* is the introducer, the case is tried out of doors in a sanctuary, and the *basileus* when presiding at the trial takes off his crown. For the rest of the time the accused is excluded from the sanctuaries, and the law does not allow him to set foot in the Agora, but on this occasion he enters the sanctuary to make his defence. When the killer is unknown, a suit is entered against 'the doer of the deed'. The *basileus* and the tribal heads try charges against inanimate objects and animals also.

58

(1) The polemarch performs the sacrifices to Artemis of the Wild and to Enyalius, organizes the funeral contest for those who died in war, and performs the heroes' rites to Harmodius and Aristogiton. (2) Only private lawsuits fall to him, those involving metics, men of equal obligations and *proxeni*. His duty is to take these suits, divide them in ten and assign to each tribe its allotted share; the justices acting for each tribe pass them to the arbitrators. (3) The polemarch himself introduces the suits for desertion of patron and for having no patron, and, in the case of metics, for inheritance and for heiresses; and the other things which the archon does for citizens the polemarch does for metics.

59

(1) The *thesmothetae* have the power, first, to prescribe the days on which the jury-courts are to sit, and next, to assign them to the officials; the officials abide by their assignment of the courts. (2) They act as introducers for all denunciations made to the people, condemnations and complaints, and for the public suits for illegal proposal and for enacting an inexpedient law, for charges against the presiding committee, charges against chairmen and generals' examinations. (3) There fall also to them the public suits in which a prosecutor's deposit is levied: for being a foreigner; for bribery by a foreigner, when someone is acquitted through bribery on a charge of being a foreigner; for malicious prosecution; for bribery; for falsely registering a man as a debtor; for falsely appearing as witness to a judicial summons; for failure to delete a discharged debtor; for failure to register a debtor; for adultery. (4) They introduce the scrutinies for all officials; claims to citizenship rejected by the deme members; and convictions forwarded from the council. (5) They also introduce the following private suits: commercial suits; mining suits; and suits against slaves, when a slave maligns a free man. They allot courts to the officials for private and public suits. (6) They ratify judicial agreements with other cities, and introduce suits based on judicial agreements. They introduce charges of perjury committed before the Areopagus.

(7) The allotment of jurors is carried out by all the nine archons, with the secretary to the *thesmothetae* making a tenth: each acts for his own tribe.

P   THE *ATHLOTHETAE* (Chapter 60)

Having completed his survey of officials appointed annually by lot our author turns to officials of other kinds, in this chapter a board which was appointed by lot but for four years, the athlothetae. *They were responsible for one of the major festivals, the Panathenaea (cf. 54.7), and he digresses from them to deal with the sacred olive oil, and with the prizes awarded for the various contests at the Panathenaea.*

60

(1) That is the position with regard to the nine archons. Ten men are appointed by lot as *athlothetae*, one from each tribe. After being scrutinized they hold office for four years: they administer the procession at the Panathenaea, and the musical contests, the athletic contests and the horse race; they are responsible for the making of the robe, and together with the council for the making of the vases, and they present the olive oil to the winning athletes. (2) The oil is collected from the sacred olives. The archon exacts it from the owners of land on which sacred olives grow, 1½ cups from each tree. Formerly the state let out the contract for collecting the crop, and if anyone dug up or cut down a sacred olive he was tried by the council of the Areopagus and, if convicted, sentenced to death. Nowadays, however, the oil is levied from the owners of the land, and the law remains but trials are no longer held: the state now obtains the oil simply from the property, not specifically from the sacred trees. (3) The archon collects the oil produced in his year of office, and hands it over to the treasurers of Athena on the Acropolis: he is not allowed to take his place in the council of the Areopagus until he has handed all the oil to the treasurers. The treasurers keep the oil on the Acropolis for the meantime, and then at the Panathenaea they measure it out to the *athlothetae* and the

athlothetae give it to the victorious contestants. The prizes are money and gold for winners of the musical contests, shields for the contest in manliness, and olive oil for the athletic contests and the horse race.

Q   ELECTED MILITARY OFFICERS (Chapter 61)

The last officials to be dealt with are the military, who held office for one year but were elected. This contrast between the military and the civilian officials was noted in the introduction to the survey of officials (43.1): there some elected civilian officials were mentioned, and we learn from chapter 54 that there was one, and had previously been another, elected secretary, but these are not mentioned again here.

61

(1) All the military officers are elected. The ten generals were formerly one from each tribe, but now are appointed from the whole citizen body. Specific duties are voted for the following: one in command of the hoplites, who commands the hoplites if they go out of Attica; one in command of the country, who guards it, and is the general who commands if there is war inside the country; two in command of the Piraeus, one for Munichia and one for Acte, who are responsible for guarding the equipment kept at the Piraeus; and one in charge of the symmories, who registers the trierarchs, conducts their challenges to exchange and introduces into court their adjudications. The other five are sent out on current business. (2) There is a vote of confidence in the generals each prytany, to decide whether they are performing their duties well. If a man is deposed, he is tried in the jury-court; and if he is convicted an assessment is made of what he should suffer or pay, while if he is acquitted he is reinstated in his office. When in command the generals have full power to arrest a disobedient man, to cashier and to impose a summary fine; but they do not normally impose fines. (3) Ten regimental commanders are elected, one from each tribe: each of these commands his tribal regiment and appoints the company com-

manders. (4) Two cavalry commanders are elected from the whole citizen body: these command the cavalry, taking five tribes each. They have the same powers as the generals have in respect of the hoplites; and they too are subject to a vote of confidence. (5) Ten squadron commanders are elected, one from each tribe, to command the cavalry as the regimental commanders command the hoplites. (6) Also a cavalry commander for Lemnos is elected, to take responsibility for the cavalry on Lemnos. (7) There is a treasurer elected for the *Paralus*, and a separate one for the ship named after Ammon.

R   CONCLUDING NOTE ON OFFICIALS (Chapter 62)

The Athenian Constitution's *survey of officials ends with notes on the method of allotment used for appointments made by lot, on stipends paid to civilian officials and on repetition of office. The assembling of the material in this chapter is probably the author's own work: section 1 reflects a change in the law but is not couched in the language of the law; the stipends to be paid to officials will have been laid down by the laws, but it is unlikely that there was a single law which listed all the stipends to be paid.*

62

(1) Formerly some of the officials appointed by lot were taken from the whole tribe, along with the nine archons, while others were distributed among the demes in accordance with an allotment made in the Theseum. However, since the demes used to sell their appointments, the second category also are now appointed by lot from the whole tribe, with the exception of the councillors and the guards, who are still assigned to the demes. (2) Stipends are paid first to the people, at the rate of one drachma for other assemblies, nine obols for the Principal Assembly. Next the jury-courts, three obols. Then the council, five obols; and the members of the prytany are given a further one obol for maintenance. The nine archons receive four obols each for maintenance, and support a herald and a piper. The governor of Salamis is given one drachma a day. The *athlothetae* dine in the town hall in the month Hecatombaeon, the month of

the Panathenaea, from the 4th onwards. The amphictyons sent to Delos receive one drachma a day from Delos. The officials sent to Samos, Scyros, Lemnos and Imbros receive money for maintenance. (3) A man may hold the military offices several times; but none of the others, except that he may serve in the council twice.

S JURY-COURTS (Chapters 63–9)

The final section of the Athenian Constitution *deals with certain aspects of the working of the jury-courts: the complicated procedure by which jurors were assigned to particular courts on particular days (63–5), the assignment of magistrates to courts (66.1), the appointment of some of the jurors as courtroom officials (66.2–3), the timing of speeches (67), the size of juries in public suits (68.1: the size of juries in private suits has already been mentioned, in 53.3), the voting procedure (68.2–69.1), the provision for a second vote in suits requiring an assessment, and the payment of the jurors (69.2). This is far from being a complete account of the trial of the major lawsuits: our author concentrates on the elaborate organization which the Athenians had developed by the second half of the fourth century, giving a detailed account of an achievement in which they took some pride (as in chapter 53 he gave a detailed account of the forty-two year-classes).*

Here as in the preceding chapters his account is presumably based on the body of laws which regulated the constitution; and it probably owes something to observation, since he could have witnessed most of the procedure which he describes even if he was a non-citizen or under thirty years old, and if he was a citizen over thirty he could have taken part in it. It is difficult to describe an elaborate procedure with which one is familiar in such a way that it will be readily understood by a reader who is not familiar with it, and the author has not always succeeded: sometimes he makes a statement that cannot be understood on the basis of the information already provided, and has to digress to add the further information which the reader needs; sometimes he fails to provide all the information which the reader needs; and the original text was not accompanied by the illustrations which accompany the notes to this translation.

From chapter 64 to the end the Greek text is incomplete and, where it survives, hard to read. For the most part the meaning is clear, if the actual words used to express it are not. The most difficult passage is 67.4–68.1: here the meaning is not certain; only two scholars have attempted to reconstruct a complete text; I translate the more recent reconstruction, by H. Hommel, and, to warn readers, print this passage in italics. At the end of chapter 69 the Greek text ends, with an elaborate flourish. It is an abrupt ending to the text; but the author was not always careful to mark the ends of sections (see pp. 29–30), and the payment of the jurors at the end of the day is a suitable topic with which to end the treatment of the jury-courts. There is no need to suppose that the conclusion of the Athenian Constitution, *like the beginning, has been lost.*

63

(1) The jury-courts are allotted by the nine archons according to tribes, the secretary to the *thesmothetae* acting for the tenth tribe. (2) There are ten entrances to the jury-courts, one for each tribe; twenty allotment-machines, two for each tribe; a hundred boxes, ten for each tribe; further boxes, in which the tickets of the men picked as jurors are placed; and two water-pots. Staves are placed by each entrance, as many in number as there are to be jurors; acorns are placed in the water-pot, the same number as the staves; and on the acorns are inscribed letters (beginning with the eleventh, *lambda*), as many in number as there are courts to be manned. (3) Jury service is open to men over thirty years old, as long as they are not in debt to the state or deprived of their civic rights. If anyone serves who is not entitled to do so, he is made the subject of an indication and is brought before the jury-court; if he is convicted the jurors assess what he deserves to suffer or pay; and, if the assessment is a money payment, the man must be placed under arrest until he has paid both the original debt which gave rise to the indication and the further sum assessed by the court. (4) Each juror has his boxwood ticket, inscribed with his name, his father's name and his deme, and with one of the letters up to *kappa*: the jurors are divided into ten sections within their tribes, approximately equal numbers to each letter. (5) When the *thesmothetes* has drawn lots

for the letters which are to be assigned to the courts, the attendant takes them and fixes its allotted letter to each courtroom.

64

(1) The ten boxes inscribed with the letters up to *kappa* are placed in front of each tribe's entrance. The jurors drop their tickets into the box which bears the same letter as is on their ticket, and then the attendant shakes the boxes and the *thesmothetes* draws one ticket from each. (2) The man whose ticket is drawn is called the inserter, and he inserts the tickets from his box in the column on the allotment-machine which bears the same letter as the box: he is drawn by lot so that the inserting shall not always be done by the same man and provide scope for dishonesty. There are five columns on each of the machines. (3) The archon, when he has inserted the cubes, draws lots on the machine for the tribe. There are bronze cubes, some black and some white: according to the number of jurors to be picked, white cubes are inserted to such a number that there shall be one cube for five tickets; and the black are added on the same principle. When the archon draws out the cubes, the herald calls the men who have thereby been picked. The inserter is included in the number of men picked as jurors. (4) The juror responds to the call, draws an acorn from the water-pot, and displays it with the letter upwards, showing it first to the archon in charge. On seeing it, the archon places the juror's ticket in the box which bears the same letter as the acorn, so that the juror shall go to the court to which he has been assigned by lot and not to whichever court he wishes, and no one shall be able to assemble men of his own choice in a court. (5) Beside the archon stand as many boxes as there are courts to be filled, each bearing the letter which has been allotted to one of the courts.

65

(1) The juror shows his acorn again to the attendant, and then goes inside the barrier. The attendant gives him a staff of the same colour as the court which bears the letter on his acorn, so that he is obliged to go into the court to which he has been assigned: for if he goes

into another he is exposed by the colour of his staff. (2) Each of the courtrooms has a colour painted on the lintel of the entrance. The juror takes his staff and proceeds to the court which is of the same colour as his staff and has the same letter as is on his acorn. When he goes in, he is given an official token by the man who has been appointed by lot to that office. (3) After entering in this way the jurors retain their acorn and staff and take their seats in the court. The inserters give back the tickets of the men who have been rejected in the allotment. (4) The public attendants from each tribe bring the boxes, one to each court, containing the tickets which bear the names of the men from that tribe who are serving in each court. They hand over the boxes to the men, five in number, appointed by lot to return the tickets to the jurors in each court, to enable them to use the tickets to call up the jurors and pay them their stipend.

66

(1) When all the courts have been filled, there are placed in the first court two allotment-machines, bronze cubes on which are painted the colours of the courts, and further cubes on which are inscribed the names of the presiding officials. Two of the *thesmothetae* picked by lot drop in the cubes: one drops the cubes with the colours into one machine, and the other drops the cubes with the officials' names into the other. Whichever official is drawn first, the herald announces that he is to have the court which is drawn first, and the second official is to have the second court, and so on, so that no one shall know in advance which of the courts he is to have but each shall have the one allotted to him. (2) When the jurors have gone in and have been distributed among all the courts, the official presiding in each court draws one ticket from each box, so as to obtain ten, one from each tribe. He drops these tickets into another empty box, and draws out five of them, one for the water-clock and four others for the ballots, so that no one shall arrange who is to be in charge of the water or the ballots and there shall be no dishonesty in these matters. (3) The five who are not drawn take charge of the instructions which specify how the jurors are to receive their stipend and where each tribe is to stand when they have given their verdict: the

The Athenian Constitution

intention is that the jurors shall be separated and receive their pay in small groups, rather than many men being enclosed in the same space and getting in one another's way.

67

(1) After these arrangements have been made, the trials are called: when private matters are being decided, private suits are called, four in number, one from each of the categories prescribed by law (and the opposing litigants swear to keep to the point at issue); when public matters are being decided, public suits, and each court tries one suit only. (2) There are water-clocks with tubes as outlets: water is poured into these, and speeches in trials must keep to the time thus measured. There is an allowance of ten measures in suits for more than 5,000 drachmae, and three measures for the second speech; seven measures and two measures respectively for suits up to 5,000 drachmae; five measures and two measures for suits up to 2,000 drachmae; six measures for adjudications, when there is no second speech. (3) The man appointed by lot to take charge of the water-clock closes the tube whenever the secretary is about to read out a law or testimony or the like. However, when a trial is being timed by the measured-out day, he does not stop the tube for the secretary, but there is simply an equal allowance of water for the plaintiff and for the defendant. (4) *This day is measured out according to the length of days in Posideon, since this allowance can be applied to the days of the other months. Eleven jars are used, and are distributed in fixed proportions: the juror in charge of the clock sets aside three jars for the voting, and the opposing litigants take equal shares of the remainder. Previously plaintiffs used to be eager to compress the defence into a very small share of the time, so that the defendants had to make do with whatever water was left; but now there are two separate containers, one for the plaintiffs and one for the defendants. (5) In earlier times the juror in charge used to take out some of the water as an allowance for the second vote. The full measure of the day is used for those public suits where there is an additional penalty of imprisonment, death, exile, loss of civic rights or confiscation of property, or an assessment has to be made of what the offender should suffer or pay.*

68

(1) *Juries for public suits consist of five hundred and one men,
and these try the lesser suits; when a court of a thousand is needed
for the greater suits, two panels are combined in the* heliaea; *for
the greatest suits, three panels are combined to make fifteen hundred.*
(2) There are bronze ballots, with an axle through the middle, half
of them hollow and half solid. When the speeches have been made,
the men appointed by lot to take charge of the ballots give each
juror two ballots, one hollow and one solid, in full view of the
litigants so that no one shall take two solid or two hollow. Then
the man appointed by lot for this task takes the staves, in exchange
for which each juror when he votes is given a bronze token with
the three-obol design (when he gives this up he is paid three
obols). The purpose of this is that all shall vote: no one can be
given a token unless he casts his vote. (3) There are two jars in
the court, one of bronze and one of wood, capable of being dis-
mantled so that no one may secretly insert ballots. The jurors cast
their votes in these: the bronze jar counts and the wooden does not;
the bronze one has a pierced attachment through which only one
ballot can pass, so that one man cannot cast two votes. (4) When
the jurors are ready to vote, the herald first makes a proclamation,
to ask whether the litigants object to the testimonies; objections are
not allowed once the voting has begun. Then he makes another proclamation: 'The hollow ballot is for the litigant who spoke first,
the solid for the one who spoke afterwards.' The juror takes his
ballots together from the stand, gripping the axle of the ballot and
not showing the contestants which is the hollow and which is the
solid, and drops the one that is to count into the bronze jar and
the one that is not into the wooden.

69

(1) When all the jurors have voted, the attendants take the jar that
is to count, and empty it on to a board which has as many holes
as there are ballots, so that the votes that matter may be laid out
for easy counting, both the hollow and the solid. The men in charge
of the ballots count them on the board, the solid and the hollow

separately; and the herald proclaims the numbers of the votes, the hollow for the plaintiff and the solid for the defendant. Whoever has the greater number wins; if they are equal the defendant wins. (2) Then the assessment is made if one is needed. The vote is taken in the same way; the jurors give back their three-obol token and take back their staff; for speeches on the assessment each litigant has a half measure of water. When the jurors have completed the trials prescribed by the laws, they receive their stipend, each in the division to which he is assigned by lot.

THE EPITOME OF HERACLIDES

This is the beginning of a set of excerpts made at an unknown date from a fuller set of excerpts made in the second century BC from the collection of constitutions (see p. 10). It is an incompetent piece of work: the amount of detail declines as the summary proceeds; section 7 ought to appear between sections 4 and 5; in compressing the material the excerptor sometimes fails to indicate that he has moved on from the subject of the previous sentence to a new subject. I give here a literal translation, in which I deliberately abstain from clarifying the ambiguities and correcting the errors of the original, and from converting its disjointed sentences into readable continuous prose.

FROM HERACLIDES' BOOK ON CONSTITUTIONS: THE ATHENIAN

(1) The Athenians had a monarchy from the beginning. When Ion settled with them, they were first called Ionians. Pandion, who was king after Erechtheus, divided the sovereignty among his sons. They persisted in strife. Theseus made a proclamation and reconciled them on equal and similar terms. He went to Scyros, and met his death when Lycomedes, afraid that he would make the island his own, pushed him over the cliffs; later, at the time of the Persian Wars, the Athenians brought back his bones. After the Codridae they no longer appointed kings, because the kings seemed to be given to luxury and soft. Hippomenes, one of the Codridae, wanted to refute the slander, so when he caught an adulterer with his daughter Limone, he killed him by yoking him to his chariot, and shut her up with a horse until she died. (2) When the supporters of Cylon took refuge at the altar of the goddess on account of the tyranny, Megacles and his followers killed them: they expelled those who had done the deed as men under a curse. (3) Solon, when legislating for the Athenians, also made a cancellation of debts, which is called the Shaking-off of Burdens: when some men complained to him about the laws, he went abroad to Egypt. (4) Pisistratus was tyrant for thirty-three years and died in old age. Pisistratus's son Hipparchus was childish, amorous and fond of the arts, Thessalus was younger and bold. Being unable to eliminate this tyrant they killed his brother

Hipparchus. Hippias's tyranny became very bitter. And he introduced the law about ostracism, which was enacted because of those who behaved like tyrants: among others, both Xanthippus and Aristides were ostracized. (5) Ephialtes made his own fields available to any one who wished to take the fruit, and from his fields he gave dinner to many. (6) Cleon took over and corrupted the government; and even more those after him, who filled all men with lawlessness. And they eliminated no less than fifteen hundred men; when they had been overthrown, the leaders were Thrasybulus and Rhinon, who was a gentleman. (7) Themistocles and Aristides. And the council of the Areopagus had many powers. (8) And they take charge of the streets, so that no one shall build to obstruct them or extend balconies over them. Likewise they appoint the Eleven, to take charge of the men in the gaol. Also there are nine archons, six *thesmothetae*, who undergo a scrutiny and swear that they will exercise their office justly and will not take bribes or else will dedicate a golden statue. The *basileus* administers things to do with sacrifices and military affairs.

NOTES

Many matters not explained here are explained in the Glossary and Subject Index and the Index of Persons and Places, below.

The Athenian Constitution

1 Cylon's *coup* was in one of the years 636, 632, 628, or 624; since Epimenides' 'cleansing' of the city by the expulsion of the Alcmaeonids included the removal of the bones of the dead, that must be placed significantly later, after Draco's legislation but before Solon's reforms. The opening words of chapter 2 will refer to the *coup* and its immediate aftermath.

2.1 Throughout his history the author thinks of the citizen body as divided into a small upper class and a large lower class: he uses various terms to denote the two classes.

2.2 Probably the sixth-parters had not arrived at that state as defaulting debtors given a second chance (as used to be believed) but had accepted a dependent position in the insecurity of the dark age between the Mycenaean and the classical periods, when it was better to belong at a low level and be protected than to be free and unprotected: as life became more settled, the less successful sixth-parters risked enslavement for debt, the more successful came to resent their dependent status. Almost certainly there were also in Athens, though our author does not mention them, some farmers who were neither dependent on an overlord nor overlords themselves. 'Champions of the people' will be encountered frequently in the *Athenian Constitution*: chapter 28 contains a list of champions of the people and of the notables.

3.1 'Before the time of Draco' was inserted when the 'Constitution of Draco' was inserted in chapter 4: see pp. 23–4, 32–3.

3.2–3 It is acceptable that the military powers of the king should have been transferred to a separate polemarch (either because of a king's weakness, as the author believes, or because in some other circumstances the king's power was thought to be excessive), and that his civil powers should have been transferred to a separate archon; but we should expect the archon to be instituted before rather than after the more specifically named polemarch. Acastus was Medon's son, so the author is right to say that the choice between the two is not of great chronological importance. According to 57.1, the *basileus* alone, not the *basileus* and the polemarch, was responsible for the traditional festivals, and that appears to be nearer to the truth.

3.4 If Draco gave Athens her first written laws, and the *thesmothetae* existed before Draco's laws (which is likely if not certain), their duty cannot have been that stated here, even though it is the duty which we should infer from their name. Probably they were judicial officers.

3.5 The buildings mentioned have not been found, but new evidence suggests that the town hall was to the east of the Acropolis; and the Epilyceum ought to be associated with the Lyceum, further to the east, rather than with a man called Epilycus. The *basileus* for some of his business used the Portico of the Basileus, at the north-west corner of the Agora; but that was not built before c.550, perhaps not until after 480. See map 3, p. 168. For judicial procedure in early Athens see on 9.1.

3.6 What is said of the Areopagus is to be repeated in 4.4 and 8.4; the Areopagus lost its function of guarding the laws in 462/1 (25.2).

4.1 Later Greeks believed that Draco had given Athens a complete code of laws but that all his laws except those on homicide were superseded by Solon's laws (7.1); his laws were renowned for their severity, and were sometimes alleged to have prescribed the death penalty for almost every offence. Probably he set in writing Athens' current practice; and possibly what he prescribed for every offence was not the death penalty but total loss of rights, so that an injured party whose charge was upheld might exact whatever retribution he thought fit; Solon's laws will then have set limits to the retribution which might be taken for different offences. For the law of homicide see 57.3–4.

4.2 It is a sign of later invention that estates are assessed in monetary terms, when Solon in 594/3 was to assess in terms of produce (7.3–4), and that a higher qualification should be laid down for generals (who became the most important officers of state in the fifth century) and cavalry commanders than for archons and treasurers.

4.3 Athens was given a council of four hundred by Solon (8.4), a council of five hundred by Cleisthenes (21.3): the odd one above the round hundred was characteristic of Athenian juries (53.3, 68.1). Allotment came to be used for nearly all civilian appointments (43.1); classical Athens set a minimum age of thirty for officials (see 30.2, 31.1, 63.3), and was able to enforce a stricter rule against repetition of office (62.3); the democracy did not punish councillors for absence (but the oligarchs of 411 envisaged punishment: 30.6) but paid them for attendance (62.2). Monetary fines are an anachronism;

the classes are those which were to be defined and given political significance by Solon (7.3–4).

4.5 See 2.2–3: probably this cross-reference was inserted with the 'constitution'.

5.2 Some have doubted the link between Solon's reforms and his archonship, and have thought that the reforms make better sense after the troubles of 13.1–2 and nearer to the time of the tyranny; but Draco earlier and Cleisthenes later are not said to have legislated as archons, so the link should not be doubted when it is asserted. For Athens as the mother city of the Ionians see pp. 39–40.

5.2–3 The poems quoted do not prove that Solon was 'of the middle sort' or that he fought and disputed 'against each side on behalf of the other', but only that he associated himself with the poor in their grievances against the rich; but Solon does display impartiality in poems written after his reforms, quoted in chapter 12. Solon was related to Pisistratus: that and the fact that he was appointed archon prove that he was a member of the aristocracy. Plutarch (*Solon*, 2) claims that Solon's father reduced his estate through acts of charity and Solon therefore took to trade: in what survives of Solon's poems there is nothing to confirm this, and it may be that passages in which he associates himself with the poor have been misunderstood and embroidered on; but it is possible that passages now lost would confirm his impoverishment and his trading activity. In section 3 our author refers to 'these poems', and then gives a single quotation which does not support what he wants to support: possibly he has been careless in excerpting from a source which did include a more pertinent quotation. In the quotations, some editors prefer 'tottering' or 'aflame' to 'being slain', and 'all things' to 'these things'.

6.1 There did in fact remain a few circumstances in which enslavement for debt was still possible in classical Athens. Cancellation of all debts, of whatever kind, was often advocated by revolutionaries in later centuries but is hard to credit in Athens in the early sixth century: Solon may have cancelled some other debts, but the quotation in 12.4 suggests that his main cancellation was of the obligations of the sixth-parters, thereby making them the unencumbered owners of the land which they farmed. (For Androtion's denial that Solon cancelled debts see on chapter 10.) Solon did nothing else to make small farms more viable, and the danger of debt, if not of enslavement, remained for the future (see on chapter 16).

6.2–4 Democratic writers represented Solon as naive but innocent, others represented him as guilty; there is no suggestion that any Greeks rejected the whole story. Plutarch (*Solon*, 15) names as the culprits ancestors of men who were prominent at the end of the fifth century, Conon, Alcibiades and

Callias, and our author says that the story was told in connection with 'men who were later reputed to be of ancient wealth': in the time of Solon it can hardly have been possible to raise capital and acquire land in exchange for it at short notice, and probably the story was invented later to discredit the families named by Plutarch. For Solon's refusal to become tyrant see 11.2 and the quotation in 12.3.

7.1 For Draco's ordinances see on 4.1. Plutarch (*Solon*, 25) refers to the inscription of the laws on wooden axles (*axones*): probably that word and *kyrbeis* were applied to the same objects, a collection of wooden beams, revolving on axles, set perhaps vertically in a frame (see figure 1, p. 123); they survived substantially intact to the second century BC, and fragments still existed in the time of Plutarch. Draco's laws were inscribed on similar objects. The Portico of the Basileus was not built until after the time of Solon (see on 3.5): Solon's laws were perhaps placed originally on the Acropolis, moved to the Portico by Ephialtes in 462/1, and moved from there to the town hall at the beginning of the fourth century, when a revised law code was placed in the Portico. The ancient stone on which the archons stood to swear their oath was in front of the Portico; 55.5 specifies more closely the offence after which a dedication was required.

7.2 According to Herodotus (I.29), the period was only ten years, and was linked with the ten years of Solon's absence from Athens (11.1).

7.3 Except in the 'Constitution of Draco' (4.3) it is not stated elsewhere that the classes already existed: the basis of assessment, and the naming of the highest class only with reference to that basis, suggest that the other names were already in use as a rough and ready classification of the citizen body and that Solon set apart the highest class, defined the basis of classification and gave the classes their political significance. Some editors prefer 'the other offices' (in contrast to the assembly and jury-courts) to 'the major offices'. The treasurers of Athena were appointed from the first class (8.1, 47.1), the nine archons from the first two (at any rate by the fifth century: 26.2); an assembly had always existed, and probably even the poorest citizens had always been entitled to attend; for the jury-courts see 9.1.

7.4 Possibly 'measures' of dry and liquid produce were treated as equivalent; or possibly a more sophisticated method was used and (for example) four *metretai* of olive oil were regarded as equivalent to one *medimnos* of barley. It has often been supposed, but cannot be proved, that later the classes were redefined in monetary terms: if this was done, the basis of assessment will have been property rather than income. The statue must be of Anthemion: possibly the error should be blamed on a copyist, and 'of Diphilus' after 'statue' deleted. The implication of the last sentence seems to be that the

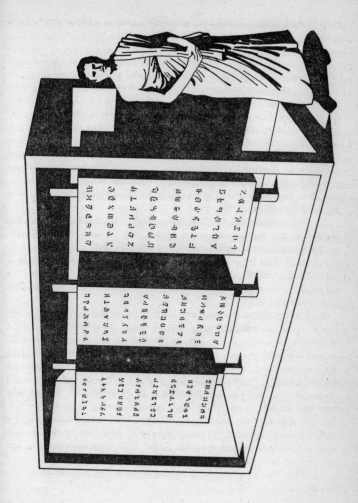

Figure 1   A possible reconstruction of the *kyrbeis*

rules limiting particular offices to members of particular classes were retained in theory but came to be ignored in practice.

8.1 Aristotle's *Politics*, in contrast to our text, asserts that Solon made no change in the election of officials by the people (II. 1273b–1274a, III. 1281b): if Solon's laws survived to the fourth century and after, the truth should have been ascertainable, and it is more likely to have been ascertained for this book than for casual references in the *Politics*. Reference to the treasurers (see 47.1) should perhaps be seen as appealing to a familiar fact to confirm an unfamiliar one, not as implying that Solon's law on the archons was no longer accessible. If Solon did introduce allotment from an elected short list (to improve the opportunities of the rich non-aristocrats to gain appointment), this will have given way to direct election under the tyranny, and have been reinstated in 487/6 (22.5); we do not know when allotment replaced election for the first stage.

8.2 That good evidence survived for procedure before Solon is much less likely; but it is not incredible that appointments should have been made by the Areopagus (and perhaps ratified by the assembly).

8.3 On the four tribes see pp. 39–40. If the quotations from obsolete laws are authentic, and if coinage had not yet been introduced (see on 10.1–2), they indicate that by the time of Solon uncoined silver was being used as a means of payment.

8.4 The council of four hundred has been suspected, but unnecessarily: the Areopagus as a council of ex-archons would remain dominated by the Well-born for some time to come, so the creation of a new council would be useful if Solon wanted to end the aristocrats' monopoly of power. Like the later council of five hundred (45.4), this council was to prepare business for the assembly (Plutarch, *Solon*, 19): probably Solon required both it and the assembly to hold regular meetings. On the Areopagus see 3.6: there may have been records which included bare lists of punishments, but it is unlikely that the reasons were not known or stated when the punishments were inflicted. Solon's law of 'denunciation' may be accepted (perhaps as a regularization of an already existing procedure), but in Solon's time offences against the state are more likely to have been formulated as in 16.10 than as here.

8.5 This law was notorious: its authenticity has been doubted, but unnecessarily.

9.1 For the ban on loans against personal security see 6.1. Previously the right to take legal proceedings had been limited to the injured party and where necessary his next of kin: Solon distinguished between 'public' and 'private' lawsuits (see 'Lawsuits' in Glossary); there are some instances in classical Athens where proceedings were initiated by an official body, but there was never a regular police authority responsible for detecting and prosecuting offenders. Previously judicial decisions had been given by individual officials or by the Areopagus; Solon provided for appeal against the decisions of individual officials to a court which probably was called the *heliaea* and consisted of a judicial session of the assembly; by the mid fifth century appeals had become so frequent that the procedure was regularized, and in most cases the official held a preliminary inquiry and then referred the suit automatically to a jury-court, thought of as a subdivision of the *heliaea*, in which he presided (see 56.6).

9.2 For alleged ambiguity in Solon's laws see 35.2 (with further information on the law of inheritance). The point that Solon must not be blamed for the later democracy is made also in Aristotle's *Politics*, II. 1273b–1274a.

10.1 A chronological distinction has been read, wrongly, into what was originally a logical distinction between the Shaking-off of Burdens and Solon's other reforms.

10.1–2 The author attributes to Solon three 'increases': of the bushel, from that associated with king Pheidon of Argos to a larger unit; of weights, from a mina of seventy drachmae to a mina of one hundred drachmae; of coinage, from a two-drachmae standard coin to a four-drachmae standard coin; he adds that Solon had the coins struck slightly below their nominal weight, so that sixty-three minas' worth of coins would weigh sixty minas. Plutarch (*Solon*, 15) repeats from Androtion the statement that Solon increased the measures, and did not cancel debts (6.1) but in effect reduced them, by an 'increase' in the coinage which divided the mina into one hundred drachmae instead of seventy. In fact Athens' bushel was larger than Pheidon's; in Athens' weight system the mina was divided into one hundred drachmae while in some other systems the same mina was divided into seventy drachmae, and all Athens' units of weight were slightly increased between the time of Solon and the time of the *Athenian Constitution*; almost certainly there was no coinage as early as Solon, but Athens did begin (in the mid sixth century) with a two-drachmae coin and later changed to a four-drachmae coin; the coins were not made heavier to match the change in weights, but were slightly overweight in the sixth century and slightly underweight (as stated in the text) in the fourth. Probably Solon did legislate for the use of standard measures and weights, and was wrongly supposed by later writers to have changed Athens' standards; he had nothing to do with Athenian coinage, but there was a tendency later to attribute all of Athens' institutions to Solon, and since the same names were used for coins as for the corresponding weights it was particularly easy to imagine that he had dealt with coins as well as with weights.

11.1 For the ten years of Solon's travels see on 7.1; problems about the men he is said to have met on his travels are lessened if we recognize that his travels need not have ended when the ten years were over.

11.2 See the quotations from Solon's poems in chapter 12.

12.3 The words 'bad' and 'good' could be used both of a man's moral character and of his social standing: here, and again in section 4, they are used in the latter sense, of the lower and upper classes respectively.

12.4 The 'markers' had presumably been planted by the overlords in the land farmed by the sixth-parters, as a sign of their interest in the land and its produce: by uprooting the markers Solon freed the sixth-parters from their obligations. We do not know how many Athenians sold abroad as slaves Solon redeemed, nor how he found them and induced their purchasers to part with them.

13.2 An earlier Damasias had been archon in 639/8. Probably this Damasias was a descendant of his, and therefore one of the Well-born, objecting to the admission of commoners to office; and the solution finally adopted was a guarantee that half (and not less) of the short list each year should be commoners. Whether the two classes other than the Well-born are authentic is doubtful (see pp. 39–40): the word translated 'rustics' is derogatory, unlike the words used elsewhere of the class of Farmers.

13.3 We are given three grounds of discontent: that the Shaking-off of Burdens had made the rich less rich, that the change in the constitution had made the Well-born less powerful, and that some men (perhaps especially rich commoners) were ambitious. However, we should expect the grievance which won Pisistratus most of his support to be that the poor were still poor.

13.4 Herodotus gives the factions regional characteristics only, and gives Pisistratus's faction what was probably its correct name, the men 'beyond the hills' which encircled the plain of Athens (rather than the men of the Diacria, the hilly north-east of Attica: his own home was at Brauron, on the east coast). In the *Athenian Constitution* the factions have distinct political ideologies: the language in which this is expressed is redolent of the fourth century, but it appears to be true that Pisistratus appealed particularly to the unprivileged, that the majority of the Well-born lived in the plain of Athens, and that Megacles was capable of cooperating either with Lycurgus or with Pisistratus.

13.5 In 'those ... not of pure Athenian descent' the author is probably thinking of the immigrant craftsmen whom Solon had attracted to Athens with the offer of citizenship. By the time of the review there was also a second class of immigrants, the tyrants' mercenary soldiers.

14.1 Since the time of Cylon (chapter 1) there had been several periods of war between Athens and Megara, with both cities claiming the island of Salamis (cf. 17.2). The war in which Pisistratus was general was the last; after it Spartan arbitrators approved the possession of Salamis by Athens. 561/0 is not the thirty-second but the thirty-fourth year by inclusive counting from Solon's archonship, 594/3: probably the upheavals mentioned in 13.1–2 led the author or his source to miscount and lose two years.

14.2 It is possible that Solon lived to 560/59 and witnessed Pisistratus's first *coup*, but this story (of which differing versions are found) is probably an invention.

14.3 On the nature of Pisistratus's rule cf. 16.2.

14.4 'Fifth' is a correction of the papyrus's 'twelfth', made to obtain consistency in the *Athenian Constitution*'s chronological data.

15.2 17.3 reveals support from Argos.

15.3 'Pallenis' refers to the temple of Athena Pallenis, in Pallene, on the main route from Marathon (where Pisistratus landed) to Athens.

15.4 Thucydides (VI.56, 58) claims that under the tyranny the citizens bore arms to take part in the Panathenaic procession, and were disarmed only after the murder of Hipparchus (chapter 18): we cannot tell which is right. If the *Athenian Constitution* is right, we should perhaps prefer an alternative version which locates the armed parade in the Anaceum, the sanctuary of Castor and Pollux, east of the Acropolis: there is no evidence for any Theseum, let alone one capable of accommodating an armed parade, before the fifth century.

16.2 On the nature of Pisistratus's rule cf. 14.3 (first period of tyranny). Presumably the tax of section 4 provided for the loans.

16.3 A ruler is no doubt safer if his subjects are not seriously under-employed, but busy peasants are not necessarily a sign of oppression, and Pisistratus may have been more interested in helping poor farmers to earn their livelihood (in particular, perhaps, by enabling them to change from cereals to the slower-yielding but more profitable olives and vines; and it is possible that he confiscated some land from his rich opponents and gave it to the poor).

16.4 Probably no clear distinction was made between the tyrant's revenue and the state's revenue. Thucydides (VI.54) writes of Pisistratus's sons imposing a produce tax of a twentieth: probably 'tithe' is a general term, not specifically implying a tenth, and Pisistratus like his sons exacted a twentieth.

16.5 These travelling justices were abolished probably on the fall of the tyranny and revived in 453/2 (26.3). Probably the lesser disputes which they settled would not otherwise have been brought to Athens, but Pisistratus was substituting representatives of the central authorities for the local aristocrats.

16.7 From Hesiod (late eighth century) onwards the age of Zeus's father Cronus is represented as a golden age. We do not know when or by whom this label was applied to Pisistratus's rule, but perhaps it was in the later stages of the tyranny.

16.8–9 Contrast 22.1. Tyranny was an extra-constitutional phenomenon, and it is no doubt true that for the most part Pisistratus governed Athens according to the already existing laws, working through the existing political institutions, and for instance retaining the nine archons but ensuring that men whom he did not trust were not appointed (here, however, the tyrants seem to have abandoned Solon's method of appointment for direct election: see on 8.1). A fragment of the archon list, inscribed on stone in the fifth century, shows Hippias and members of the leading families of Athens holding office after Pisistratus's death.

16.10 The author describes this law as mild because in his own day 'without rights' (*atimos*) commonly meant 'without political and judicial rights'; but earlier it had meant 'outlawed', with the implication that the outlaw might be killed with impunity. The original law quoted can hardly be later than the time of Solon; the preamble points to a subsequent reaffirmation of the original law.

17.1 Pisistratus will have been about seventy-five at his death.

17.2 For the war with Megara cf. 14.1: probably the war to which Solon urged the Athenians was fought before 594/3 and was not the war in which Pisistratus was general. As for the story that Solon was Pisistratus's lover, years of birth are more relevant than years of death, and since Solon was born *c.*630–625 and Pisistratus *c.*605–600 the story is, as far as chronology is concerned, entirely plausible. The two men were in fact related (see on 5.2–3).

17.3 Information from other sources suggests that Thessalus and Hegesistratus were different men: Thessalus like Hippias and Hipparchus was a son of Pisistratus by his first, Athenian wife; Iophon and Hegesistratus were his sons by Timonassa (to whom he was duly married – but in the fourth century marriage with a non-Athenian was no longer permitted under Athenian law: see on 26.4). For the battle of Pallenis see 15.3.

18.1–2 The description of Hipparchus as amorous leads us to expect the story as told by Thucydides, in which it is he who was in love with Harmodius: our author has failed to reconcile conflicting sources. Thucydides insists that it was not Hipparchus but Hippias who was the eldest son and reigning tyrant, and (a claim with which not everything in his account is compatible) that the personal grievance was the sole reason for the plot: since tyrant was not a formal office the *Athenian Constitution* may be right to write of shared power, but Hippias will have played the dominant part; and the men who supported Harmodius and Aristogiton will not have shared their personal motive.

18.2–3 The narrative is largely in agreement with Thucydides, but there are differences of detail.

18.4 'The story' is found in Thucydides: see on 15.4.

19.1 For Thucydides the tyranny became cruel only after the murder of Hipparchus: the *Athenian Constitution* has already had one degeneration, in 16.7 after the death of Pisistratus.

19.3 For 'below Parnes' the papyrus has 'beyond Parnes'; but that is geographically wrong, and our author is not likely to have made the mistake.

19.4 The previous temple had been burned in 548/7, and probably the Alcmaeonids took the contract long before 514 and by 510 had completed the work or had done enough to earn Delphi's gratitude. According to Herodotus, they did a more lavish job than they had contracted to do, and the oracle was for that reason willing to pass on their message; in the *Athenian Constitution* this is combined with a fourth-century version of the story, in which they took the contract after their failure at Lipsydrium and borrowed or embezzled the building funds to hire mercenaries.

19.5 Our manuscripts of Herodotus give the Spartan's name as Anchimolius, but the form given here is more probably correct. The Athenians believed that a people called the Pelasgians had built the (in fact, late Mycenaean) wall round the Acropolis; at the west end of the Acropolis was a sacred enclosure called the Pelargikon; and Pelargikon and Pelasgikon were supposed (probably wrongly) to be alternative versions of the same name. Hippias was besieged on the Acropolis.

19.6 For the total length of the tyranny the papyrus has 'forty-nine years'; but on our author's arithmetic the interval from 561/0 to 511/0 should be reckoned as fifty years, and in any case what is needed here is not that whole period but the number of years of tyranny during the period, on his arithmetic thirty-six years.

20.1 Herodotus does not say that Isagoras was a 'friend of the tyrants'; probably this is our author's inference from the fact that he was an opponent of Cleisthenes, whose family claimed the credit for expelling the tyrants. Cleisthenes' 'getting the worse of the struggle' was exemplified in the election of Isagoras as archon (21.1).

20.2 Isagoras 'fell behind' when the assembly approved Cleisthenes' proposals for reform (probably as archon Isagoras presided but was powerless to resist a clear majority). The curse is that imposed on the men responsible for killing Cylon's supporters (chapter 1).

20.3 'Seven hundred' households is in agreement with Herodotus, but is scarcely credible. The council which Cleomenes tried to dissolve was probably the council of four hundred (8.4). Herodotus adds two later attempts by Sparta to intervene in Athens: a military expedition to reinstate Isagoras, *c.*506, which was frustrated by disunity within the army (V.74–7), and a proposal to restore the tyrant Hippias, *c.*504, which was rejected at a meeting of Sparta's allies (V.90–96).

21.1 The material in chapter 21 follows chapter 20 because it is derived from a different source, not because the author disagreed with Herodotus on the order of events: it was probably the approval of Cleisthenes' reforms by the assembly which prompted Isagoras to call in Cleomenes (see on 20.2), though there will not have been time to put the reforms into effect until after Cleomenes' withdrawal (see on 22.2). We do not know what Isagoras's position was in the latter part of 508/7, but there is no evidence that he was replaced by another archon.

21.2 The four old tribes and their subdivisions remained (see section 6), but only the new units were to be of political significance: Cleisthenes 'mixed up' the people by cutting across old channels of influence and so lessening the dependence of the ordinary citizens on the aristocracy.

21.3 For the council of four hundred see 8.4; for the thirds of a tribe see p. 40. It would of course have been possible to create twelve new tribes which were not identical with the old thirds.

21.4 In Cleisthenes' new system the basic unit was the deme, of which there were 139, varying in size. Demes, mostly but not always neighbouring demes, were grouped in thirds, and one third from each region was put together to make a tribe, in such a way that the tribes were approximately equal in population. If, as our author suggests, each third consisted entirely of demes from one region, the thirds must, like the demes, have been unequal in size; but a good case has been made by P. Siewert, *Die Trittyen Attikas und die Heeresreform des Kleisthenes* (*Vestigia*, 33; Munich: Beck, 1982), for the view that the thirds were equal in size, and each was based on one region but did not consist entirely of demes from one region. The more eccentric groupings of demes suggest that Cleisthenes was interested in breaking old associations (in which, as it happened, the Alcmaeonids were at a disadvantage); in the new system the Alcmaeonids were well placed, with their homes near the city in three tribes and the coastal strip towards Sunium where they probably had land and dependants in the same three tribes; it does not seem to have mattered whether the different thirds of the same tribe were near to one another. By the fourth century it had become normal for an Athenian to be identified by his father's name and his deme name (for instance, Demosthenes son of Demosthenes, of Paeania, the orator): that the deme name was intended to replace the father's name and to assist the assimilation of newcomers into the citizen body is probably a fourth-century guess. Cleisthenes was believed to have enfranchised some men (Aristotle, *Politics* III. 1275b), probably those who had been disfranchised in the review of 13.5, but since his proposals made him more popular than Isagoras his main appeal must have been to those who already had votes, and the attraction of the new system was probably its provision of an apparatus for local government.

21.5 Very little is known about the *naucrariae* (see Glossary). One of the *Atthides* stated that Cleisthenes did not abolish them but made them fifty in number instead of forty-eight; we cannot tell which is right, but *naucrariae* are not heard of again, and if they survived now they are not likely to have survived beyond Themistocles' enlargement of the navy (22.7).

22.1 Other texts, including 16.8, claim that Pisistratus kept to Solon's laws, and it is likely that on the whole these other texts are right. Ostracism is first mentioned here, left in the air, and resumed in section 3: probably this is due to the author's careless compression of his material.

22.2 For 'eighth' the papyrus has 'fifth', but 504/3 is occupied by another archon and leaves too many years before 490/89. Some have thought that this year saw a revision of Cleisthenes' dispensation, but more probably it took several years to work out the details of his organization and 501/0 was the first year in which the new council of five hundred met and other appointments based on the ten new tribes could be made. Previously generals had been appointed *ad hoc* for campaigns outside Attica: now there were to be ten generals each year; as we see from Herodotus's account of the battle of Marathon (VI.105–17), at first the polemarch remained formal commander-in-chief of the army but the effective command was transferred to the generals; after Marathon the polemarch is not found with the army again, and by the mid fifth century the nine archons were routine officials (see 26.2) while the generals were the most important men in Athens.

22.3–4 Another text, derived from the *Atthis* of Androtion, states in words very close to those of the *Athenian Constitution* that ostracism was instituted at the time of its first use; but most probably that text misrepresents Androtion, and he said what the *Athenian Constitution* says and indeed is the *Athenian Constitution*'s source here. As a means of preventing tyranny, ostracism would be unreliable, since a potential tyrant with popular appeal might be able to ensure that a majority of votes was cast against someone else (and ten years of exile had not prevented Pisistratus from returning and recovering the tyranny). It would, however, be an effective means of letting the people choose between rival political leaders, as Cleisthenes and Isagoras had been: that is how it was used after the first three instances, until, probably in 416, it was expected that the voters would choose between Nicias and Alcibiades but the supporters of those two combined to produce a majority against Hyperbolus; it may well be that Cleisthenes was thinking of such situations rather than, or as well as, the threat of tyranny. Certainly it is unlikely that ostracism should have been introduced specifically in order to eliminate Hipparchus son of Charmus. Since this first victim was a Pisistratid (probably a grandson of Hippias) and Hippias had come to Marathon with the Persians, and the second was an Alcmaeonid and the Alcmaeonids were suspected of disloyalty at Marathon, and the third was another 'friend of the tyrants', it appears that ostracism was first used to remove men who were under suspicion but not demonstrably guilty after Marathon.

22.5 For the appointment of the archons see on 8.1: possibly after the fall of the tyrants men were elected to the board of archons but given a particular post on the board by lot (since Herodotus, VI.109, states that the polemarch serving at Marathon had been appointed by lot). That the short list comprised as many as five hundred is most unlikely: in the fourth century the short list picked by lot comprised one hundred (8.1), and the reference here to the demes suggests that the author's mind has strayed to the council of five hundred, for which the demes served as constituencies.

22.6 The third victim of ostracism is unknown: probably our author, wishing to avoid a monotonous list, left out a name which meant nothing to him. Xanthippus is said to be 'unconnected with the tyranny': he was married to an Alcmaeonid, and one man who wrote two lines of verse to vote against him perhaps thought that he was tainted with the Alcmaeonid curse; but he had successfully prosecuted Miltiades, the hero of Marathon, shortly after the battle, and it is incredible that this prosecution should have succeeded if the prosecutor was generally regarded as belonging to the Alcmaeonid set. We should probably think of a three-cornered personal rivalry between Xanthippus, Aristides and Themistocles, with Themistocles as the successful man who was not ostracized (though he is known to have attracted votes in the 480s).

22.7 Herodotus (VII.144) and many other writers mention Themistocles' shipbuilding programme. The *Athenian Constitution* is unique in writing of a secret plan in accordance with which money was lent on trust to rich individuals: it may be true that individuals were made responsible for the building of individual ships, but it is incredible that the plan should have been kept secret. Different texts give different numbers of ships: in fact Athens seems to have had seventy in 490 and two hundred in 480.

22.8 The papyrus has 'fourth year', but 480/79 is less plausible for the recall of the ostracized and is occupied by another archon. Hipparchus did not return, and was condemned as a traitor; the others did return. Many editors change 'within' to 'not within' or 'outside', but probably the text is sound and should be taken to mean that men ostracized were not to go nearer to the Persian Empire than a line joining those two points.

23.1 The ascendancy of the Areopagus, 'not by any formal decision', is probably an inference from Ephialtes' reform of the Areopagus in 462/1 (chapter 25). Plutarch (*Themistocles*, 10) quotes an alternative version of the story, with Themistocles responsible for providing the money before Salamis: probably the version of the *Athenian Constitution* is the older, and the alternative is a reply to it. This was one aspect of a propaganda battle in which Themistocles and Cimon were linked with alternative interpretations of Athens' recent history.

23.2 If 'despite the opposition of the Spartans' is correct, our author disagrees on this point with Thucydides (I.95), but that is not a fatal objection to the text though some editors have thought it to be so; Diodorus of Sicily (XI.50) reports a debate in Sparta which unexpectedly ended in a decision not to contest Athens' naval leadership.

23.3 Most texts (including, I believe, 28.2) represent Aristides and Themistocles as opponents, but there are some which place the two men on the same side, and for the period after the Persian Wars I believe this divergent tradition is correct. In this period Cimon (26.1) was the most successful Athenian politician, and after the foundation of the Delian League (sections 4–5) Athens does not seem to have made further use of Aristides and Themistocles. Themistocles was ostracized about 470: for his subsequent fate see on 25.3–4. Aristides' uprightness was notorious, but Themistocles was renowned for political skill no less than for military prowess.

23.4 After the Persian Wars Sparta did not want any cities north of the Isthmus of Corinth fortified: Themistocles went to Sparta and prevaricated while the Athenians rapidly rebuilt their walls; then Aristides and a third Athenian joined him in Sparta and they acknowledged what had been done (Thucydides, I.90–93, and other texts).

23.4–5 Our author refers to Athens' foundation of the Delian League, a naval alliance to continue the war against the Persians, after the Spartan commander Pausanias had made himself unpopular (Thucydides, I.94–7). Most of the allies paid tribute (*phoros*) in cash each year. The material given here makes the League a full offensive and defensive alliance, and the sinking of lumps in the sea probably implied that the alliance should last until they rose again, that is, for ever.

24.1 That Aristides gave the advice attributed to him here is unlikely;

and it appears from Thucydides (II. 14–17) that the Athenians did not migrate to the city on a large scale until forced to do so by the Peloponnesian War, which began in 431.

24.2 Samos (until 439), Chios and Lesbos continued to supply ships when all other members of the League were paying tribute in cash; but probably Athens interfered with the freedom of her allies as opportunity and need arose, and there was no time when all these three but no others remained free from interference in the respects stated. In general Athens encouraged democracy among her allies and Sparta encouraged oligarchy among hers.

24.3 It is alleged in Aristophanes' *Wasps*, 707–11, that Athens has a thousand tribute-paying allies (a gross exaggeration), who could provide maintenance for twenty thousand Athenians. Our author or his source has been ingenious in collecting figures wherever they could be found: even where the individual figures for recipients of pay are correct, it should be remembered that not every man was paid for every day in the year. Jury pay, probably in the early 450s, seems to have been the earliest instance of state payment for civilian duties (see 27.3–4). The repeated '700 overseas' is almost certainly a scribal error, but the correct figure is irrecoverable. 'When the Athenians subsequently organized their military affairs' (a correction of the papyrus's text which not all editors accept) introduces figures which are presumably to be interpreted as peacetime quotas of some kind: they are certainly too small for Athens' forces in the Peloponnesian War. The ships sent to collect the tribute are a mystery, as it was normally the duty of the allies to send their tribute to Delos (after 454, to Athens), but no satisfactory correction has been proposed. For entertainment in the town hall see on 3.5. The orphans are the sons of citizens fallen in war, and were maintained at the state's expense until they came of age. The guardians of prisoners are the Eleven (52.1).

25.1 If the text is sound, the author has reckoned not from 480/79 (as in 23.5, 27.2) but from 479/8, so 'seventeenth' should perhaps be corrected to 'eighteenth'. It is not easy to understand how the masses should have 'increased' in a period of 'decline': the 'decline' harks back to the view of Athens after the Persian Wars given at the beginning of chapter 23, while the view of Ephialtes' reform given here is from a source favourable to the reformers, and probably this accounts for the awkward conjunction. Little is known about Ephialtes. The reform of the Areopagus is ascribed to him and a man called Archestratus in 35.2; other texts link Pericles with Ephialtes, and the reform ascribed to Pericles in 27.1 has probably been wrongly separated from Ephialtes' reform. Ephialtes, like Aristides (23.3), is said to be upright: the same claim is not made for Pericles in chapter 27, though his admirers made it.

25.2 The men eliminated were probably retiring archons, who if they passed the examination at the end of their year of office became life members of the Areopagus. For guardianship of the constitution see 3.6, 4.4, 8.4. The powers taken away are described as 'accretions' in the *Athenian Constitution*, as part of the established order in texts hostile to the reform (e.g. Plutarch, *Cimon*, 15); possibly over the years the Areopagus had used its title of guardian of the laws, and the prestige of its members, as pretexts for enforcing the law in new ways without formal authorization. Ephialtes will have taken from the Areopagus that title, and judicial functions of political importance: the scrutiny of officials before they entered office (55), the examination of officials after they retired from office (48.4–5, 54.2), and any checks on their conduct during their year of office (see 43.4; 61.2, 4; 45.2; 48.3); and also the trial of 'denunciations' of major offences against the state (8.4, 43.4). Extra business for the jury-courts will have made the final version of judicial procedure described in the note on 9.1 necessary now if it had not been introduced already; after Ephialtes' reform, the council of five hundred became important as an administrative and judicial body (see 45–9), as well as being the body which prepared the assembly's business, and its standing committee, the prytany (43–4), was perhaps created now. The judicial powers which the Areopagus retained concerned homicide (57.2–4) and certain religious offences (see, for example, 60.2).

25.3–4 Themistocles was a member of the Areopagus, having been archon in 493/2; he and Ephialtes had links with the same set of men; and after his ostracism of *c*.470 he was condemned for collaboration with the Persians, probably after a denunciation to the Areopagus, and then fled to the Persians. He cannot have been a partner of Ephialtes, since almost certainly his condemnation was some years before Ephialtes' reform; but it may be his condemnation, and the acquittal of their opponent Cimon (27.1), which provoked Ephialtes' attack on the Areopagus. The story of Themistocles is probably an addition to the original text of the *Athenian Constitution* (see pp. 32–3); but the last sentence of the chapter, with its unexplained 'too', will be part of the original text. A speech of the late fifth century (Antiphon, *On the Murder of Herodes*, 68) cites Ephialtes' murder as an instance of an unsolved crime: perhaps it was known that Aristodicus was the actual killer and assumed that he must have acted on behalf of a group of Athenians.

26.1 'Slackness' is a metaphor based on the stringing of a bow or musical instrument: for Aristotle the ideal was a mean between excessive slackness and excessive tautness, for some other writers 'manly' tautness was preferable to 'effeminate' slackness. 'Demagogue' (people-leader) as a term for political leaders was coined in the late fifth century: for Aristotle, but not for other writers, it is always a hostile term to be used of extreme democratic leaders;

in the *Athenian Constitution* it is used always of democrats but not always pejoratively (in the translation I use the English word 'demagogue' only when it is pejorative). What is said of Cimon is difficult: he was born *c*.510, and was prominent in the 470s and 460s as Athens' commander in the campaigns of the Delian League; Ephialtes opposed his desire to help Sparta against a revolt of her serfs, the helots; probably in his absence Ephialtes' reforms were enacted and because of Ephialtes' success Sparta dismissed the Athenian troops; and on returning and failing to upset Ephialtes' reforms Cimon was ostracized; he died on campaign soon after his return to Athens ten years later. The comment here reads as an aristocrat's *apologia* for failing to prevent the victory of the democrats, and it looks as if our author has misplaced a comment which belongs to the beginning of Cimon's career. 'Better sort' at its first appearance refers to the upper classes, but it is implausible that they particularly should have been hit by casualties in war, and at its second appearance the word is used in a moral sense. In the fifth century partial mobilization was a matter of selection (for fourth-century practice see 53.7), so it is arguable that 'better' men were more likely than 'worse' to serve and to be killed or wounded.

26.2 It was a criticism levelled by Aristotle at extreme democracies (e.g. *Politics* IV.1292a) that they did not adhere to the 'laws' (thought of as having more validity than the enactments of a particular state at a particular time) but decided everything by 'decrees' of their assemblies (see 41.2 and Glossary). If the archon of 457/6 was the first to hold office under the new rules, the new rules must have been enacted not later than the previous year: the author has not worked this out.

26.3 See 16.5. The number thirty suggests one for each of Cleisthenes' thirds of a tribe. For the fourth-century change to a board of forty working in Athens see 53.1.

26.4 Previously the son of a citizen father would become a citizen irrespective of his mother's origin, and there were some distinguished sons of non-citizen mothers (for instance, Cleisthenes, Themistocles, Cimon). If, as is likely (see on 42.1), a man had to be born in wedlock to be entitled to citizenship, the effect of the law will have been to limit citizens in their choice of wives, rather than to limit the size of the citizen body. Probably in the fifth century, as the number of metics (non-citizen immigrants) increased, mixed marriages had become more frequent and therefore less acceptable, and so Pericles insisted that the benefits of Athenian citizenship should be available only to those who were fully entitled to them. This law was ignored or annulled during the Peloponnesian War, reaffirmed afterwards, and reinforced in the fourth century by a law which forbade mixed marriages.

27.1 Pericles was one of the men elected to prosecute Cimon in 463/2, at the end of Athens' siege of Thasos, on a charge of taking bribes to spare Macedon. Probably the trial was before the Areopagus, in Cimon's examination at the end of his year of office; it was alleged that Pericles was induced by Cimon's sister to treat Cimon gently; Cimon was acquitted. The reform of the Areopagus mentioned here is probably that which we associate with Ephialtes (see on 25.1). What particular contribution Pericles is supposed to have made to Athenian naval power is not clear.

27.2 On the development of democracy in the Peloponnesian War, after Pericles' death, see chapter 28: the change was not in the formal constitution but in the background and style of the political leaders.

27.3–4 Cimon's wealth, and his use of it to buy political support, were notorious. Pericles was himself rich, though not in the same class as Cimon: the story that he was using the state's wealth to do what Cimon did with his own wealth is a slander, but there is a measure of truth behind it, in that the Periclean democracy was opposed to the kind of aristocratic patronage which Cimon exercised, and Pericles may well have expected jury pay to be popular with voters in the assembly. More important is the fact that the democratic machinery of Athens could not work in a democratic manner unless large numbers of ordinary citizens were able to devote some of their time to making it work: jury pay was the first of many such payments, culminating in assembly pay (41.3), to compensate the citizens for the loss of earnings in the time which they devoted to the state's business. Probably jury pay was introduced soon after Ephialtes' reform of the Areopagus, during Cimon's ten years of ostracism. The papyrus's text names as Pericles' adviser Damonides of Oe: that is found also in Plutarch (*Pericles*, 9, citing the *Athenian Constitution*), so probably that is what our author wrote; but other evidence suggests that he should have written 'Damon son of Damonides, of Oa'.

27.4–5 It was in 410 or 409 that Anytus was tried and acquitted after failing to keep Pylos out of the hands of the Spartans. If that was indeed the first occasion when a jury was bribed, the Athenians were remarkably slow: in the system described in chapters 63–9 juries were made up and assigned to courts separately for each day, and bribery was difficult; but in the fifth century the six thousand who were registered as jurors each year (24.3) were divided into panels and assigned to courts once for the whole year.

28.1 It is broadly true that down to the generation of Pericles all political leaders, whether aristocratic or democratic in sympathies, were from the aristocracy themselves, whereas after his death aristocratic families tended to withdraw from active politics and new families came to occupy the foreground. Many fourth-century writers regarded the death of Pericles as the end of an era.

28.2 For Solon as the first champion of the people see 2.2. After him the papyrus's text says simply, 'The second was Pisistratus, of the well-born and notable'; but the list goes on to pair aristocratic with democratic leaders, and in the third place states positively that Cleisthenes had no aristocratic opponent, so probably the list did give Pisistratus an opponent and he has been lost in the transmission of the text. On Pisistratus and his rivals see 13.3–15.1. On the rivalry of Cleisthenes and Isagoras see 20.1–3. The pairing of Xanthippus and Miltiades is unsatisfactory, but their sons Pericles and Cimon appear on opposite sides later in the list, and *c.*489 Xanthippus prosecuted Miltiades (see on 22.6). In the next item 'respectively' corresponds to nothing in the Greek text, but I believe the intention was to make Themistocles a democratic and Aristides an aristocratic leader, even though in the main narrative (23.3, cf. 41.2) both are placed on the democratic side. Cimon (see 26.1, which delays his introduction) opposed Ephialtes (25) both in internal and in foreign policy. Thucydides (perhaps a brother-in-law of Cimon, and perhaps a grandfather of Thucydides the historian) became the leading opponent of Pericles after Cimon's death, until he was ostracized *c.*443; Pericles died in 429.

28.3 Cleon and Nicias were in fact from similar backgrounds, each being the son of the man who founded the family's fortune; but Nicias was a cautious man and one who in his political style made himself acceptable to the aristocrats, while Cleon (perhaps the first man of whom the word 'demagogue' was used: see on 26.1) relied on his ability to make extravagant and persuasive speeches in the assembly; his clothes were hitched up to make wild gesticulation easier. Both met their deaths in the Peloponnesian War, Cleon outside Amphipolis in 422 and Nicias in the disastrous end of Athens' Sicilian expedition of 415–413; Alcibiades, who opposed Nicias from *c.*421 onwards, is conspicuously absent from the list. Theramenes was an opponent of democracy, involved in setting up the oligarchies of 411 and 404 but in each case disliking the extreme oligarchy which resulted, and in the second case being put to death by the extremists (29–37): Cleophon was active in politics as early as *c.*416, was the leading democrat and opponent of Sparta from 410 to 404 (see 34.1), and had to be eliminated in 404 before peace could be made with Sparta. The two-obol grant was paid between 410 and the end of the war, probably as a daily subsistence grant to citizens who were not in receipt of any other payment from the state.

28.5 No positive achievements of Thucydides are known; Nicias was acceptable to the aristocrats but not himself an aristocrat, a cautious but successful general until in the Sicilian expedition through fear of returning unsuccessful he made total disaster certain when it might have been avoided; neither is obviously deserving of special praise. It is easy to see why the verdict on Theramenes was controversial: he may sincerely have believed in a moderate oligarchy; presumably in 404 he thought, mistakenly, that after their experience of extreme oligarchy in 411 the Athenians would not tolerate another extremist regime. It is not clear what illegalities in the democracy before 411 could be cited to justify the withdrawal of his support.

29.1 Until the Sicilian expedition of 415–413 Athens' resources were ample, but in 412 she had to use the final reserve fund set aside at the beginning of the Peloponnesian War; about the same time Athens supported a rebel against Persia, Amorges, and in 412–411 Sparta entered into a series of agreements by which Persia was to support her in the war in exchange for control over the Asiatic Greeks. The distinction between the maker of the major speech and the nominal author of a motion is without parallel: probably Pythodorus was a member of the council but Melobius (a member of the Thirty in 404/3) was not.

29.2 Thucydides (VIII.67) writes, probably mistakenly, of a drafting committee of ten. 'With a view to the city's safety' on this occasion no doubt meant what it said, but it had become a standard formula to cover discussion of any subject for which urgency could be claimed.

29.3 The oligarchs claimed that they were not introducing a dangerous novelty but returning to the good old days: hence the reference to Cleisthenes' 'traditional' laws and his 'democracy'. Whether a text of Cleisthenes' laws was known to exist is disputed: probably it was not known in 411 whether a text existed or not.

29.4–5 This assembly is the assembly at Colonus of Thucydides (VIII. 67–8). First all the normal safeguards against over-hasty decision were suspended. Then positive proposals were made – by Pisander according to Thucydides (emphatically), by the drafting committee according to the *Athenian Constitution* ('they' at the beginning of section 5 certainly refers to the committee: see the first sentence of chapter 30): probably Pisander was a member of the committee, said that he was making proposals on behalf of the committee, and no one knew how far that was true. Thucydides at this point ignores the Five Thousand, who in fact played no part in the regime of the Four Hundred; our author ignores the Four Hundred, perhaps because he is to give an account of their appointment in chapter 31. Probably this assembly decided in principle that there should be a citizen body of five thousand hoplites with minimal rights (Thucydides' view of five thousand as a maximum suits the context in which he mentions it, of the oligarchs' wishes; our author's view suits the formal resolution of the assembly), and a powerful council of four hundred, and then the Four Hundred were appointed on the spot (as reported by Thucydides) and further committees were appointed to work out the details of the constitution and to draw up a register of the Five Thousand. The existence of the second committee is confirmed by other evidence, that of the first is not.

30.1 The author supposes that the constitutional committee was appointed by the Five Thousand, but Thucydides insists that, under the regime of the Four Hundred, the Five Thousand never actually came into existence: probably the constitutional committee and the committee of registrars were appointed by the assembly at Colonus, and that assembly was deemed, either at the time or very soon afterwards, to be an assembly of the Five Thousand.

30.2 We discover in 31.1 that the document in chapter 30 is a 'future' constitution, followed in chapter 31 by an 'immediate' constitution. Probably the members of the constitutional committee disagreed as to the kind of oligarchy they wanted, and the extremists took care that the 'immediate' constitution should give them all the power they wanted and saw no harm in letting the others outline a different constitution for the future (there is no reason to think that the 'future' constitution was ever put into effect). We cannot tell how much of the obscurity of the 'future' constitution is due to its compilers and how much to compression by our author. All offices (it must have been assumed) would be limited to the Five Thousand: the members over thirty would be grouped in four divisions, and (as in the cities of Boeotia) one division at a time would serve as the council (section 3); major officials would be appointed from the current council, minor officials from the remaining three divisions. A board of treasurers of the Other Gods had been created in 434/3 to take charge of a number of small temple treasuries; this board was in fact amalgamated with the treasurers of Athena in 406 (for their further history see on 47.1). The *colacretae* (7.3) were abolished and the treasuries of the Athenian state and the Delian League amalgamated under the *hellenotamiae* in or shortly before 411. The clause excluding the *hellenotamiae* from the council is puzzling: perhaps the original document said something more sensible.

30.3 Only men who have reached the age of thirty may hold office or serve in the council, but younger men are to be assigned to the four divisions so that they can exercise their full rights when they reach thirty.

30.4 We are given provision for an enlarged council, but none for an assembly of all the Five Thousand; nor are we given any provision for the transaction of urgent business between meetings of the council.

30.5 The papyrus's text reads, 'The council should be allotted ...' For the order of business compare the democratic rule in 43.6.

30.6 Where the democracy offered payments for attendance, the oligarchy threatened fines for absence: compare the 'Constitution of Draco', 4.3.

31.1 Solon's council was of four hundred, one hundred from each of the old tribes (8.4): the revolutionaries did not tamper with Cleisthenes' tribes, thirds and demes (chapter 21). The papyrus's text has 'draw up concerning the oath'.

31.2 The distinction between 'present' and 'future' within the 'immediate' constitution is presumably that between the remainder of 412/1, and 411/0 and subsequent years; but there is no indication, and no likelihood, that the Four Hundred and the officials were in fact reappointed at the beginning of 411/0.

31.3 Probably ten regimental commanders (as in 30.2 and 61.3) have been omitted either by our author or by a copyist. 'For the appointment of the generals' is not present in the Greek but has been added in translation to give the sense which I believe was intended; in the sentence beginning 'Apart from the council and the generals ...' the papyrus's text includes the phrase 'neither these nor anyone else', which makes no sense in its context. The last sentence of this chapter (which grammatically abandons the indirect speech of the rest of the two documents for direct command) is to be understood not as a part of the 'immediate' constitution but as an addition by a member of the committee who took the 'future' constitution seriously, to the effect that the committee of registrars should prepare for the eventual transition to that constitution by (listing members of the Five Thousand in their four divisions and) placing members of the Four Hundred in all four divisions. Some editors retain the papyrus's 'when it becomes possible for the citizens ...', but it is hard to see what that would mean.

32.1 Probably the constitutional documents were approved not by an assembly but by the Four Hundred: Aristomachus may have been in the chair at that meeting of the Four Hundred, or at the Colonus assembly. On the first of the two dates given (9 June) the democratic council was dissolved, and the Four Hundred took over *de facto*; on the second (17 June) the Four Hundred were formally inaugurated. Until 407 the council worked not to the calendar year of lunar months (43.2) but to a separate solar year of 365 or 366 days: thus the council's year 411/0 was due to begin on 14 Scirophorion (9 July).

32.2 The tyranny was overthrown in 511/0 (19.6). The hundred-year interval and the list of oligarchic leaders are derived from Thucydides (VIII.68): of the men named by Thucydides Phrynichus is absent from the papyrus, but this is probably a copyist's error.

32.3 Thucydides' account of the negotiations with Sparta (VIII.70–71, 86–9) does not include the Athenian proposal and the Spartan reply that are given here. The oligarchic movement began in the Athenian fleet at Samos, but the fleet reverted to democracy about the time when the oligarchy was established in Athens, so any agreement which the oligarchs might have made with Sparta would probably not have been acknowledged by the fleet.

33.1 Probably the intermediate regime kept the limitation of all political rights to the Five Thousand, but made an assembly of the Five Thousand rather than a smaller council the effective governing body of the state. We hear no more of the committee of registrars: probably all men registered as hoplites were regarded as citizens, regardless of number.

34.1 The papyrus has 'seventh year': this is a careless section, and the error may be the author's. Callias is given his deme-name to distinguish him from the archon of 412/1 (32.1–2). After Arginusae (where the Athenians made a special effort with a reserve fleet, were victorious, but owing to bad weather did not pick up corpses or survivors after the battle) not all the generals but only the eight who had taken part in the battle were condemned: in Xenophon's account the condemnation results from a malicious attack by Theramenes, but Diodorus points to a more innocent feeling of anger in Athens at the failure to pick up corpses and survivors. Diodorus and an *Atthis* place the peace offer which was rejected at the instance of Cleophon not after the battle of Arginusae but after the battle of Cyzicus, in 410.

34.2 After Aegospotami Athens could not afford to equip another fleet: the Spartan Lysander blockaded the city during the winter, and the Athenians capitulated in the spring of 404. Cleophon was opposed to the peace, and had to be eliminated on a charge of treason; Theramenes played a leading part in the peace negotiations.

34.3 Other evidence does not confirm that the peace treaty included a clause insisting on the 'traditional constitution'; but the traditional constitution was certainly discussed in 404, and it may be that the treaty stipulated that Athens was to be independent 'in accordance with tradition', that the oligarchs (perhaps not only the moderate oligarchs) argued that Athens was required to revert to what they regarded as the traditional constitution, and that the democrats replied that the traditional constitution of Athens was democracy. Theramenes was a member of the Thirty, though that is nowhere stated in the *Athenian Constitution*. The four named with him (we do not know the source of the information, nor whether it is true) were not members of the Thirty: Archinus (40.1–2) and Anytus (27.5) joined Thrasybulus at Phyle (37.1) and were influential at the restoration of the democracy; Clitophon is probably the Clitophon of 29.2 but no more is known of him; Phormisius joined Thrasybulus after he had moved from Phyle to Munichia (38.1), and after the restoration of the democracy unsuccessfully proposed a property qualification for citizenship. Probably because the influence of Plato's school survived in Aristotle's, our author does not name the leader of the extremists, Plato's relative Critias; Thrasybulus will be named in 37–8 as the leader of the returning democrats. It appears from Lysias, *Against Eratosthenes* (especially 41–78) that, although a distinction could be made in 404 between extreme and moderate oligarchs, the moderates were still oligarchic and Theramenes played an active part in setting up the regime of the Thirty. Lysander was present at the crucial assembly and put pressure on the Athenians by claiming that they had not demolished their fortifications within the time stipulated by the peace treaty. The Thirty were probably given the double task of drawing up a new constitution and ruling Athens until they had done so.

35.1 It is likely that the Thirty were appointed early in 404/3, the appointments which they made included the archon Pythodorus, and he came to be regarded as the archon for the whole year (see on 39.1 and 41.1). The papyrus's text has 'from a short list from the thousand'.

35.2 For the laws of Ephialtes see 25.2; for ambiguities in Solon's laws see 9.2. Oligarchs disliked the discretion allowed to democratic juries; the removal of the qualifications quoted from the law of inheritance would certainly lessen the possibility of disagreement, but it would not necessarily result in greater justice. Revision of the laws of Athens had been begun by the restored democracy in 410; what may have been envisaged as a short and simple task was still unfinished when the Thirty came to power; the revised code and religious calendar were completed in 399.

35.4 Our other sources indicate that it was at this point that the Thirty obtained the garrison from Sparta which our author delays until 37.2.

36.1 The Three Thousand were allowed to retain arms and remain in the city when the other Athenians were disarmed and driven out (37.2, but Xenophon places the disarming before the killing of Theramenes); they had the right to a trial before the council and were themselves used as an assembly or jury to condemn the men of Eleusis and Salamis when the Thirty wanted to provide themselves with a safe refuge.

37.1 Our other sources do not mention the occupation of Phyle until after the death of Theramenes, but on this point the *Athenian Constitution* may be right. The other sources give a dramatic account of the final clash between Theramenes and Critias in the presence of the council (for example, Xenophon, *Hellenica* II.3). The first of the two laws quoted may have been enacted when the Three Thousand were distinguished from the other Athenians, with no *ad hominem* intent; the second does appear to be an excuse for eliminating Theramenes. The fortress at Eetionea, in the Piraeus, was built by the Four Hundred in 411, and Theramenes had encouraged the men working on it to mutiny (Thucydides, VIII. 90–92).

37.2 For the disarming of the unprivileged see on 36.1, and for the Spartan garrison see on 35.4. It may be true that the Thirty felt obliged to defend the killing of Theramenes in Sparta.

38.1 The move from Phyle to Munichia was made possible by the demolition, required by Sparta at the end of the war, of the Long Walls linking Athens to the Piraeus. In the battle which followed the move Critias (see on 34.3) was killed. The Ten, who included two of the Thirty, were probably not given a mandate to seek reconciliation with the democrats, but the deposition of the Thirty may have raised false hopes. The remaining members of the Thirty retired to Eleusis (see on 36.1), and they sent their own appeal to Sparta. Lysander arranged for himself and his brother to be sent; after the Spartan new year Pausanias, who was jealous of Lysander, obtained the support of a majority of the ephors (the chief civilian officials of Sparta), and he was sent to Athens.

38.2 Other evidence confirms that the cavalry were deeply implicated in the oligarchic regime.

38.3 The deposition of the Ten and the appointment of a second Ten is not found in any other text, and is not reflected in the allusions to 'the' Ten in 39.6 and 41.2; probably the second Ten are a gross distortion of the oligarchs' half of a provisional government of twenty appointed after the reconciliation (Andocides, *On the Mysteries*, 81); Rhinon was (and Phayllus may have been) a member of the Ten who succeeded the Thirty. The *Athenian Constitution* emphasizes the part played in the reconciliation by Rhinon and Phayllus, and minimizes that played by Pausanias. Pausanias first attacked the Piraeus but afterwards encouraged the democrats there and the oligarchs in the city to seek a settlement.

38.4 Xenophon's figure of fifteen commissioners (*Hellenica* II.4), as the less obvious number, is the more likely to be correct.

39.1 The details of the settlement are found only here, and are presumably derived from an official document; but some details are left obscure, and other evidence indicates that some points have been omitted from this account. Probably the reconciliation took place early in 403/2, and Euclides like Pythodorus (see on 35.1) was appointed under the new regime, after the beginning of the calendar year: if this is so, though Euclides' name correctly dates the document to 403/2, it could not have been attached to the original document (41.1, which takes a more democratic view of the reconciliation than is taken in the preceding chapters, dates it to the year of Pythodorus). Most of the Thirty, and some of their supporters, had already occupied Eleusis (see on 38.1): hence the decision to make a semi-independent state at Eleusis for oligarchs unwilling to be reconciled with the democrats.

39.2 The Eleusinian cult of Demeter and Persephone, one of the major cults of the Athenian state, had ceremonies both in Athens and in Eleusis, and so was an obstacle to the separation of Eleusis from Athens: it was decided that for the purposes of this cult the separation was to be ignored. The alliance is that with Sparta which was imposed on Athens as part of the peace terms in 404.

39.4–5 We are not told how or with whom men who wished to emigrate to Eleusis were to register, or how men who wished to cancel their registration were to do that: the original document may have included this information.

39.5–6 Probably the *Athenian Constitution*'s list of those excluded from the amnesty is correct, though some of those listed here are omitted from other versions of the list. Those listed had to undergo and pass an examination of their conduct if they were to live as members of the community in Athens; anyone, whether on this list or not, who was accused of killing or wounding (57.3) not through an agent but in person, might be prosecuted; but otherwise there was to be a complete amnesty for acts committed before the reconciliation. An oligarch who joined the community at Eleusis would be outside the reach of the Athenian courts as long as he remained there (hence my version of the penultimate sentence of this chapter; but many editors retain the papyrus's text and take it to mean 'Then after submitting to an examination those who wished might emigrate'). What is said of the bodies conducting examinations leaves several questions unanswered (for instance, whether they were to be juries of a fixed size or assemblies of as many eligible men as chose to attend). As far as we know the amnesty worked, in the strict sense that no one was condemned on a charge to which he ought to have been immune; but, for the next half century or more, which side a man had been on in 403/2 was likely to be mentioned to his credit or discredit (with how much effect it is hard to estimate), and probably many democrats acquiesced in the loss of property rather than risk trouble in the attempt to recover it. The terms of reconciliation must have included some agreement on how the state was to be governed: in fact, after an interim government of twenty (see on 38.3) the democracy was restored; a proposal by Phormisius to restrict citizenship (see on 34.3) was defeated.

40.1 Archinus may have carried a resolution in the assembly, or may simply have persuaded whoever was in charge of the registration to accept no more names; but, however beneficial, this was a breach of the terms of reconciliation.

40.2 Many texts mention rewards for those who had supported Thrasybulus, and Archinus's opposition to generosity: at best, non-citizens who had joined Thrasybulus at Phyle may have received citizenship; the orator Lysias is the most conspicuous example of those who joined him later and did not receive citizenship. Later it was illegal for the council to condemn citizens to death (see 45.1), and probably this condemnation was illegal (or, while publication of the revised law code was pending, of doubtful legality). Another text reports a more prosaic way in which Archinus reinforced the amnesty, by introducing the *paragraphe*, a counter-suit to have a prosecution declared invalid because it infringed the amnesty. Probably both are authentic: Archinus intervened dramatically once and introduced the *paragraphe* to protect the amnesty for the future.

40.3 For the debt to Sparta, see the last sentence of chapter 39.

40.4 The community at Eleusis started hiring mercenaries; there was a battle between the forces of the two communities, followed by a reconciliation; probably the amnesty of 403 was extended to those who had been at Eleusis, with the proviso that those excluded under the provisions of 39.6 must pass an examination or go into exile.

41.1 For the date see on 39.1.

41.2 The list of changes serves as a summary of the first part of the *Athenian Constitution*. Draco, with no number, is an addition to the original list; and 'first after this', of Theseus, was probably added at the same time in a clumsy attempt to conceal the intrusion. In contrasting the Four Hundred and the restored democracy the author probably did not bother to ask with which of them the intermediate regime of 411/0 should be ranked; the Ten of 403 are mentioned without the second Ten of 38.3. On decrees (as opposed to laws) see 26.2 and Glossary; on jury-courts and democracy see 9 and 35.2; on the judicial powers of the council see 45.1. If the support of individuals has to be bought, the fewer the individuals the easier the task; but a mass of people can be corrupted *en masse*, for instance, by a promise of benefits financed from taxes paid by or property confiscated from the few.

41.3 Payment for attending the assembly (not for all, but for the first so many to arrive) was not made before 403/2; it had reached three obols a meeting by the time of Aristophanes' *Ecclesiazusae*, in the late 390s; for the level of payment in the author's day see 62.2.

42.1 For the requirement of citizen birth on both sides see 26.4; though our author does not say so, it was probably a further requirement that citizens should have been born in wedlock. If a man was judged to be free but not an Athenian, he would perhaps retain his freedom if he accepted the original judgement but lose it if he made an unsuccessful appeal.

42.2 The cadet class and its name *epheboi* are probably survivals from ancient Greek series of age-classes, found most prominently in Sparta.

42.3 The 'trainers' were gymnasts. Inscriptions show that in the fourth century 'instructors' were appointed not for the whole corps but for individual tribes: they did not have to be Athenian citizens. For state payments cf. 62.2, where these payments are not mentioned.

42.4 The theatre of Dionysus was more suitable for the display than the assembly's regular meeting-place, the Pnyx (map 3, p. 168): it was rebuilt about the time when this system of compulsory service was instituted. The gift of a shield and a spear was an innovation of the 330s: previously only war orphans were armed at the state's expense. Cadets are known to have been stationed at Eleusis, Phyle and Rhamnus.

43.1 The treasurer of the army fund was appointed by election, perhaps by analogy with the military officers (see chapter 61). The festival fund was probably instituted in the late 350s, and at first had a single elected treasurer by analogy with the army fund: he gained access to the council's supervision of Athenian finance (see 47.2), and large sums of money accumulated in his fund and were used for various purposes; in the 330s measures to lessen the power of the office included the substitution of a board of ten for the single official; a new supervisory post held by a single man was created, but is not mentioned in the *Athenian Constitution*. Probably the reference to the Panathenaea defines a single year of office (in contrast to the calendar year beginning on 1 Hecatombaeon, which was the term of office for most officials), not the four years from one Great Panathenaea to the next (see 54.7).

43.2 For Cleisthenes' council of five hundred see 21.3: individual demes were used as constituencies, providing one or more members in proportion to their size. A normal year comprised twelve lunar months of 29 or 30 days, *c.* 354 days in all; a leap year comprised thirteen months, *c.* 384 days; the scheme given here will fit a year of 354 days. It is disputed among calendar specialists whether the longer prytanies were always in fact the first four: I suspect that they were not, but that the law may have stated what the *Athenian Constitution* states.

43.3 The Round House, on the west side of the Agora (map 3, p. 168), was built in the second quarter of the fifth century: possibly the prytany as a standing committee of the council was instituted by Ephialtes in 462/1, and the Round House was then built to accommodate it. There were about seventy-five festival days in the year which were holidays for the council. The assembly now had four regular meetings in each prytany (but at an earlier date the Principal Assemblies will have been the only regular meetings), and probably could have additional meetings if necessary; the four meetings were not necessarily held in the order given in the text. The council-house was adjacent to the Round House, but the council's business sometimes required it to meet elsewhere. The original council-house was built possibly *c.* 500, possibly at the same time as the Round House; *c.* 400 a new council-house was built and the old one became a depository for records.

43.4 For the vote of confidence cf. 61.2, 4. For denunciations see 8.4: charges of major offences against the state, originally tried by the Areopagus, were after Ephialtes' reform in 462/1 made to the council and assembly (see on 25.2); the case could be, and after *c.* 360 regularly was, referred to a jury-court for the final decision.

43.5 There had not been an ostracism (see chapter 22) since *c.* 416. Complaints could also be made about some offences connected with festivals. Possibly the text is misleading, and complaints could be made in every prytany, not only the sixth.

43.6 It is hard to believe that there were enough supplications to occupy the whole of one assembly each prytany: presumably when any supplications had been heard other business could be transacted. What is said of the preliminary vote is condensed to the point of obscurity: see Glossary.

44.1 Our author probably includes in 'the state's funds' the sacred treasures which were kept in various sanctuaries. In the fifth century there had been a single state treasury, but in the fourth the state's secular funds were distributed among various spending authorities (see 48.2). When it was believed that Cleisthenes' thirds of tribes were far from equal in size, evidence was seen in some inscriptions that a more equal subdivision was also made, and it was thought that the thirds mentioned here were based on the more equal divisions; but if the conclusion adopted in the note on 21.4 is correct there is no need to look for thirds other than those of Cleisthenes.

44.2–3 In the fifth century the *prytanes* and their chairman presided at meetings: the presiding committee was instituted probably in the 380s, and probably in order to share out the work of the councillors more evenly. A ballot was required for those decisions of the assembly for which a quorum also was required, but most votes were by show of hands, probably without a precise count.

44.4 This would be better placed in the latter part of chapter 43. It is not clear how much latitude is denoted by the clause 'in whatever way the people see fit'; for the extent to which appointment was based on the ten tribes, see on 61.1. Preliminary resolutions of the council have not yet been explained, but are to be explained in 45.4.

45.1 There remained other ways in which offenders could be put to death without the sentence of a jury-court: Eumelides ought to have argued not that only a jury should sentence to death but that the council should not do so. However, it is hard to find a time when the council lawfully exercised the absolute power of which it is here said to have been deprived: probably it acquired judicial powers by Ephialtes' reform in 462/1 and these powers were limited from the start (in the fourth century the council in fact had absolute power to impose fines up to 500 drachmae but had to refer a case for a second hearing in a jury-court if it wanted a heavier penalty: this applies to section 2 also); the story will have been invented or misapplied to explain a fictitious reduction in its powers. The punishment envisaged for Lysimachus is death by *apotympanismos*, perhaps by being fastened to a plank and slowly strangled by a collar round the neck, or perhaps by being beheaded (in which case we should translate 'the man who returned from the block').

45.2 This denunciation is technically different from that in 43.4, but many offences committed by officials could be dealt with by either means and it is not always easy to distinguish which is being used.

45.3 On scrutinies cf. chapter 55. In the case of councillors, probably the council's rejection was subject to a right of appeal or automatic reference but its acceptance was final.

45.4 It was standard Greek practice, in states of various political complexions, for the deliberations of the citizen assembly to be controlled to some extent by those of a smaller council. Athens gave its assembly the greatest possible freedom: the council had to approve a subject for debate if the assembly was to reach a decision on it, and the council's preliminary resolution could, but did not have to, embody a positive proposal; but as long as the subject for debate had been approved, any citizen could speak, and could propose an amendment or alternative motion. For the charge of illegal proposal see 59.2.

46.1 Probably the author originally wrote of triremes only (warships with three banks of oars, and one man to an oar); in the 320s Athens began to build quadriremes and quinqueremes (ships with two banks of oars, and more than one man to an oar), and quadriremes were added here when the text was revised: see p. 32. There was a board of overseers of the dockyards, not mentioned in the *Athenian Constitution*, which exercised immediate control. The council's award was a gold crown: Androtion was prosecuted for proposing that the council of 356/5, of which he was a member, should receive its award although it had not satisfied the shipbuilding requirement; after that the voting of the award was deferred to the following year.

46.2 It is not made clear whether the council's responsibility was for buildings already standing, buildings under construction or both; but there is no evidence of its concern for existing buildings apart from those which it used. Some editors change the end of the sentence to read, '... and, if the people convict him, it [the council] hands him over to a jury-court', but this would be procedurally stranger than the papyrus's text. Presumably, as in chapter 45, the case would go to a jury-court only if the council wanted a penalty beyond its own competence.

47.1 By the fourth century the criteria for membership of the property-classes (7.3–4) had become so unrealistic that a poor man might find himself in the highest class, and/or the laws basing eligibility on class were not enforced and a man who wished to hold any office would simply claim that he belonged to an appropriate class. On the treasurers and their appointment see 8.1. In 406 the treasurers of Athena and the treasurers of the Other Gods were amalgamated (see on 30.2); in 385/4 the two separate boards were revived; from the 340s there was again a single board, but entitled treasurers of Athena. The statue of Athena is the cult statue in the Parthenon, made by Phidias between 447/6 and 438/7; the Victories are gold statues.

47.2 For the financial officials who joined in the council's supervision of the sellers see 43.1: it was perhaps when a board replaced the single official in charge of the festival fund that the treasurer of the army fund too was given a share in this supervisory function. Presumably the sellers did the detailed work and the council formally voted the award of the contracts. 'Seven years' is derived from fourth-century mine contracts: the figure in the papyrus is probably 3, wrongly repeated by a scribe from the previous category. Whitewashed boards, on which the text was written in charcoal, were the normal medium for temporary notices.

47.3–4 For the ninth prytany of the year cf. 54.2.

48.1 Precautionary imprisonment, until a debt was paid, is to be distinguished from penal imprisonment, which was beyond the council's powers (45.1); in one instance imprisonment was obligatory (63.3). The council pursued defaulters through another board of ten, the exacters (*praktores*).

48.2 The allocation of funds to different spending authorities replaced the use of a central state treasury early in the fourth century.

48.3 These auditors are distinct from the annual auditors, treated in 54.2.

48.4–5 Our author separates the general examination from the audit at the end of a man's year of office because the examiners were members of the council but the annual auditors were not. 'In market hours' is the least unsatisfactory of several guesses: the papyrus is indecipherable at this point. For 'thirty days' many editors read 'three days'. The papyrus has 'who introduce cases' for 'who give verdicts', and 'if they receive an accusation' for 'when they receive an accusation', but these are probably scribal errors. For the statues of the tribal heroes cf. 53.4: presumably each examiner sat by the hero of one tribe (probably not his own), to receive charges against members of that tribe.

49.1 For 'and are unmanageable' some editors prefer a phrase which is thought to mean 'but run away'.

49.2 There was a fixed quota of 1,000 cavalry in the late fifth and fourth centuries: the 1,200 of 24.3 includes 200 mounted archers.

49.3 For the robe for Athena's cult statue and prizes for the Panathenaea see 60.1; for the Victories see 47.1. The papyrus has 'plans [for buildings?] and the robe', which some editors accept.

49.4 Grants to war invalids are attested from the sixth century; grants to all impoverished invalid citizens were probably introduced in the second half of the fifth. In the early fourth century the grant was one obol a day; at all times it was less than an unskilled but able-bodied man could earn, and less than was paid for the performance of civic duties (62.2). Earlier in the fourth century the council had had two treasurers.

50.1 For the allocation of funds by the receivers see 48.1–2. Thirty minas a year would cover only minimal repairs.

50.2 Dancing-girls as well as musicians should have been covered by the law. Presumably the city magistrates were concerned with entertainers available for casual hire, and the richer citizens made their own arrangements to have entertainers regularly available to their households.

51.3–4 The increase in the number of corn-guardians was probably made in the 320s, when Greece suffered from a serious shortage of corn, and there are indications that the original version of the *Athenian Constitution* did not mention the increase (see p. 32). Greek city states were not much interested in controlling trade, but Athens like many states was dependent on imported corn, and in this case the state did see fit to intervene.

52.1 Common criminals (*kakourgoi*, 'wrongdoers'), and men who had been deprived of but persisted in exercising civic rights, could be brought to summary justice by three procedures: by 'delivery', by *ephegesis* (bringing the authorities to the accused and requiring them to arrest him) and by 'indication' (see 63.3 and Glossary). In the last case the accused could, but did not have to, be placed under arrest, and it is possible that the Eleven were responsible when he was arrested and the *thesmothetae* when he was not.

52.2 'Monthly' lawsuits were those for which there was a streamlined procedure, and an opportunity to initiate proceedings every month (as there was not for many kinds of suit): all were private suits. The introducers (each responsible for suits against defendants of two tribes) were instituted after the mid 340s, and monthly suits at the same time or slightly earlier; other monthly suits were handled by the *thesmothetae* (59.5). Suits for a dowry were available certainly to the head of a woman's own household, after divorce or the death of her husband, and possibly also to a husband when a promised dowry had not been paid. Interest of more than 1 per cent per month could be charged, but could not (except, presumably, when the money was borrowed to finance trade in the Agora) be enforced through a monthly suit. 'Battery' seems to have been a less serious charge than 'wounding' (57.3). 'Friendly loans' were made by a plurality of people, for repayment in regular instalments but without interest.

Notes

53.1 For the earlier history of the Forty see 16.5, 26.3 (deme justices). Chapters 56–9 mention other private suits, in addition to those handled by the introducers, which were outside the province of the Forty. Four of the Forty were assigned to each tribe (not their own), and handled suits against defendants of that tribe (see the end of section 2).

53.2 The public arbitrators were not quite public officials, but resembled private arbitrators, chosen by the mutual consent of the disputants: possibly for that reason they had first to attempt an agreed settlement, and only if they failed in that to pronounce a verdict.

53.3 For the odd one juror cf. 68.1: juries voted by ballot, with a precise count, and the purpose of the odd one was to avoid a tie.

53.4 Men were registered at the new year after their eighteenth birthday (42.1), so their sixtieth birthday fell in their forty-second year on the registers. In a world in which years were not numbered in series, the forty-two heroes of the year-classes were a convenient device for ensuring that men remained liable to serve for precisely forty-two years. For the heroes of the tribes see 21.6: by the second half of the fourth century the statues stood on the west side of the Agora, opposite the old council-house (map 3, p. 168), and their base served as a state notice board (see also 48.4).

53.5 There will have been different numbers of arbitrators in different tribes, but probably they were assigned to a tribe other than their own, as nearly equally as possible, to handle suits against defendants of that tribe. The obligation was to complete a case that was begun even if this could not be done within the arbitrator's year of service; we do not know how long an absence, for how good a reason, was necessary for exemption.

53.7 In the fifth century a partial mobilization was achieved by selection (see on 26.1); in the second half of the fourth, by mobilizing a stated age-range.

54.2 Cf. 48.3 (interim auditors), 48.4–5 (examiners). For 'These are the men who' the papyrus has 'These are the only men who'. Strictly 'examination' refers to the more general check on officials' conduct, and our author should have written 'introduce the audit into the jury-court', but the meaning of 'examination' was often extended to include the audit. The minimal penalty for 'misdemeanour' (*adikion*) suggests that this was a minimal offence, perhaps an accounting error with no intent to defraud. For the significance of the ninth prytany of the year, see 47.3–4. In the first half of the fourth century men who were fined were immediately treated as defaulters on debts to the state, and were deprived of their civic rights and could be imprisoned until they paid; but under a law of the 350s they were treated as men under contract to pay by the ninth prytany.

54.3 The first secretary mentioned was the principal state secretary. Until the mid 360s he was elected from the members of the council, to serve for one of the ten prytanies of the year but not that of his own tribe; thereafter he was appointed by lot from the citizen body, to serve for a year (the title given here, which seems more appropriate before the change, is not found until after it; he also, before the change and after it until the 320s, bore the title 'secretary of the council'). Secretaries did lose their original prominence in the headings of public documents, not because they became less important, but because from 407 the council worked not to its own year but to the calendar year, which was sufficiently identified by the name of the archon.

54.4 The reader might suppose that the first secretary was responsible for decrees and the second for laws; but in fact the first was responsible for both and is named in the preambles of both, and in the second half of the fourth century two additional secretaries are found, the one mentioned here and a presumably parallel secretary 'in charge of decrees'.

54.5 In the ancient world it was impossible to issue copies of documents to men attending a meeting, so the Athenians appointed a secretary to read documents at meetings of the council and assembly: this was considered a skilled job, so (unlike most civilian jobs: see 42.1) was filled by election, but the usual rule that appointment was for one year only (62.3) still applied. Similarly each of the jury-courts had a secretary to read documents (67.3).

54.6–7 Sacred as well as secular matters were the state's concern: some religious appointments were hereditary (for instance, the position of the Eumolpidae and the Heralds in the Eleusinian cult: 57.1), others were included in the ordinary range of state appointments (for instance, the treasurers of Athena: 8.1, 30.2, 47.1). Various titles are found: there were several boards of *hieropoei*, of which our author mentions two; from the 330s if not earlier there was a separate board for the Panathenaea (on that festival, but not on its *hieropoei*, see chapter 60).

54.7 The papyrus has no noun with 'occurs in the same', but probably the meaning is that given in the translation; it appears to be true that none of the four major festivals administered by this board fell in the same year. The festival added in 329/8 is an obvious addition to the original text (see p. 32): the name Hephaestia fits the traces on the papyrus but there is no other evidence for a quadrennial festival of Hephaestus; a quadrennial festival of Amphiaraus, at Oropus, was revived in 329/8 but Amphiarea does not fit the traces; perhaps Amphiarea was originally written but was corrupted, and a scribe misguidedly corrected to a name which made sense to him.

54.8 Salamis, though in Athenian hands since the sixth century (see 14.1, 17.2), was never incorporated in the Athenian state but was ruled as subject territory (as were Eleutherae, in the far north-west of Attica, and, when it was in Athenian hands rather than in Boeotian or independent, Oropus, in the north-east). Piraeus was one of the demes of Attica (see 21.4), but as the harbour town of Athens was important to the Athenian state as a whole.

Notes

Several demes had a local festival of Dionysus, some including dramatic performances as the state festivals of Dionysus did (56.1, 57.1). The last sentence may refer to a published list of governors of Salamis.

55.1 'So-called' distinguishes the nine archons from the one entitled archon, and from 'archons' in the sense of officials in general (see Glossary). For their earlier history see 3.2–4, 8.1, 22.5, 26.2. The addition of the secretary, we do not know when, made the nine into a standard board of ten, one of whom could be appointed from each tribe: despite the text's 'in turn' there is no evidence for regular rotation of the different offices among the tribes.

55.2–4 On the scrutiny of the archons cf. 45.3. Three stages in the history of the scrutiny seem to be envisaged: (a) in the council only; (b) when the Athenians were afraid mainly of unjust rejection, so two hearings were required but the second was a formality when there was no accuser; (c) when they realized that there was also a danger of unjust acceptance, so two serious hearings were required in every case. It would, however, be a strange reform which added a second hearing in every case but made it a formality in some cases: possibly the formal vote when there was no accuser belongs in fact to the sole hearing, before Ephialtes' reform of 462/1 when that took place in the Areopagus (see on 25.2), and a single reform substituted two serious hearings, in the council of five hundred and a jury-court. The questions about family cults and family tombs would confirm that a candidate was a genuine Athenian; support for parents in their old age was required by the laws of Solon. In early Athens, when the archons were drawn from a limited class (at first the aristocratic, later the rich), the men appointed will have been well known and the scrutiny will have been a matter of formal confirmation rather then genuine inquiry.

55.5 For the stone and the oath cf. 7.1: the more precise formulation of the offence calling for a dedication, given here, is the more likely to be correct. Written evidence replaced spoken in judicial proceedings from about the 370s, but witnesses still had to appear in person, and those who denied evidence attributed to them had to do so on oath.

56.1 It is uncharacteristic that the three senior archons chose their assistants: this may be a survival from the archaic state.

56.2 The proclamation will be another survival, since in classical Athens the archon had little opportunity to break or enforce this promise: possibly Solon, after proclaiming his Shaking-off of Burdens (chapter 6), enacted that future archons should guarantee the security of property.

56.3 The richer citizens were required to support the state not only by paying taxes but also by undertaking public duties at their own expense as liturgies (see Glossary). A man could not be required to perform a particular festival liturgy more than once, or to perform more than one liturgy in two years, and the archon's instructions were probably to appoint for the current year the richest men who were not then exempt; but the system provided an opportunity for politically valuable display, and many men performed more liturgies, more expensively, than they need have done. The archon was responsible for the Great Dionysia, with its tragic, comic and dithyrambic (choral) contests, and for the Thargelia, with its dithyrambic contests. There were also tragic and comic contests at the Lenaea, but that was one of the festivals of the *basileus* (57.1). For the festival at Delos see 54.7; the pilgrimage was annual.

56.4 The Asclepia fell on the day before the procession from Athens to Eleusis for the concluding ceremonies of the Mysteries. The change in the Dionysia is part of a general change in the financing of festivals made in the 330s.

56.6 The preliminary inquiry, where the official who was to preside in the court checked that a case was in order, is a descendant of the official's independent verdict against which under Solon's law a disappointed litigant could appeal to the *heliaea* (see on 9.1). Normally prosecutors were penalized if they withdrew from the case or failed to obtain one fifth of the jury's votes. Adjudication of a guardianship was to settle a dispute between potential guardians of an orphan; the suit 'for displaying to public view' was to secure the production of an object to enable the claimant to lay hands on it.

56.7 See the text of the law, quoted on p. 28.

57.1 The Eumolpidae and the Heralds were two clans in which many offices connected with the Eleusinian cult of Demeter and Persephone were hereditary. The Eumolpidae were of Eleusinian origin; the Heralds were not, and gained their stake in the cult when the Athenian state as a whole took an interest in it. The statement here about traditional festivals is closer to the truth than that in 3.3.

57.2 Because of the pollution arising from homicide, when a charge was lodged with the *basileus* he made a solemn proclamation that the accused was banned from the places and activities specified in the homicide law (see section 4).

57.3–4 The word for 'kill' originally implied violence and bloodshed, so killing by poison is mentioned separately; 'wounding' was presumably more serious than the 'battery' of 52.2; arson was included perhaps because of the danger to life. The Areopagus tried those who were charged with killing a citizen, intentionally, by their own act and unlawfully; the court at the Palladium those charged with killing a non-citizen, or with killing anyone unintentionally or through the act of another; the court at the Delphinium those charged with killing but lawfully. The charge for which reconciliation was possible, if the victim's kin agreed, was unintentional killing: the accused stood his new trial in a boat offshore so that he should not return from his exile prematurely.

57.4 The fifty-one men are members of the Areopagus, styled *ephetai*: some editors restore that title to the text here; the number fifty-one was probably included in the original text but is absent from the papyrus. It was possible to charge an animal or an inanimate object with homicide: in that case the court comprised the *basileus* and the heads of the four old tribes, with no other jury.

58.1 The sacrifice to Artemis celebrated the victory over the Persians at Marathon in 490; Enyalius was a god of war. For Harmodius and Aristogiton see chapter 18: their cult was comparable to the honours for men who died fighting for Athens, and was made the responsibility of the polemarch for that reason.

58.2 On the different categories of non-citizen, see Glossary. The machinery for handling private lawsuits (chapter 53) depended on the tribe of the defendant: non-citizens did not belong to a tribe, and so suits against them had to be specially assigned to tribes.

58.3 The first suit was against a freed slave (who would rank as a metic) who deserted his former master; the second was a suit against a metic charged with not having the citizen patron whom as a metic he was required to have.

59.2 For denunciation see 43.4: the papyrus has 'They make denunciations to the people', but that is procedural nonsense. 'Condemnations' are probably cases which the assembly referred to a jury-court after an inquiry and report (*apophasis*) by the Areopagus, a procedure used in the second half of the fourth century. For complaints see 43.5. Of the public suits which follow, the first was used against proposers of decrees of the council and assembly, and the second against proposers of laws, whether they were alleged to be illegal or inexpedient. All officials had to undergo an examination on retirement from office (see 48.4–5): it is not clear why the generals are singled out for special mention here.

59.3 The first suit was used against non-citizens posing as citizens.

59.4 For scrutinies see 55.2; for claims to citizenship, 42.1; for condemnations by the council, which had to be confirmed by a court if the council wanted a penalty heavier than a fine of 500 drachmae, 45.1–2.

59.5 Commercial and mining suits were 'monthly' suits (see 52.2–3): commercial suits, which had to concern trade to or from Attica and to be based on a written contract, were open to citizens and non-citizens on equal terms and were one of the devices tried in the mid fourth century to make

Athens more attractive to traders. The second sentence is a clumsy reiteration of what was stated in section 1.

59.6 Each city-state had its own laws and its own judicial procedures, in which non-citizens were usually at a disadvantage; but two states could enter into an agreement on the procedures to be followed in a lawsuit between a citizen of one and a citizen of the other. Normally perjury was handled by the same magistrate (but not the same jury, since juries changed every day) as the original lawsuit: we should have expected perjury before the Areopagus to be handled by the *basileus*.

59.7 The allotment of jurors is described in detail in chapters 63–5.

60.1 The robe (cf. 49.3) was used to clothe the cult statue of Athena, and was brought in procession to the Acropolis at the Great Panathenaea. The vases (of a special design) contained the olive oil presented to victors in the games.

60.2 Originally specific olive trees, supposed to be offshoots of a tree planted by Athena on the Acropolis, were regarded as sacred; the oil for the Panathenaea had to come from them, and it was therefore an offence to damage them. As some of these died, the Athenians decided instead to collect the oil simply as a tax on the land where sacred olives had grown, and so it ceased to matter if any of the sacred trees was damaged.

60.3 The contest in 'manliness' was between tribal teams, and was a contest in military prowess.

61.1 For the institution of the ten generals see 22.2; between the mid fifth century and the mid fourth the tribal basis was retained as a norm but exceptions were possible if no candidate in a tribe secured a majority vote; by the 320s the tribal basis was abandoned altogether. Regular postings for some generals are first found in the 350s; in the 320s there were the five regular postings given here; eventually all ten had regular postings. The general in charge of the symmories (see Glossary) had the same oversight of trierarchs as the archon had of *choregi*: see 56.3.

61.2 There was a regular vote of confidence in all officials, or at any rate all major officials (see 43.4): perhaps it was originally introduced for military officers and is mentioned here for that reason.

61.4 The cavalry commanders were not quite analogous to the generals, since the generals commanded the armed forces as a whole, not only the hoplites.

61.6 The island of Lemnos was an Athenian possession, settled by Athenian citizens, almost continuously from the early fifth century to the late fourth.

61.7 These two ships were used on formal state business. The name of the second was *Ammonias*: it replaced a ship called *Salaminia* c.350.

62.1 Probably appointment to the more important offices had always been made by the first method, allotment from all the candidates in each tribe. The second method involved the allotment of particular offices to particular demes within the tribe, on the assumption that the deme would fill its offices from among its own members; but sometimes, it appears, a member of another deme who wanted a particular office would pay to ensure that there were no candidates for it within the deme and it was offered outside. For the appointment of councillors see on 43.2; the guards are perhaps the five hundred guards of the dockyards (24.3).

62.2 For payment for attending the assembly see 41.3; for Principal and other assemblies see 43.4–6. Assembly pay, like most other payments, was increased to keep pace with inflation, but the rate of pay for jurors was the same in the 320s as in the 420s. For the governor of Salamis see 54.8; for the *athlothetae*, chapter 60; for Delos, 54.7, 56.3. Lemnos (61.6), Imbros and Scyros were Athenian possessions from the early fifth century to the late fourth; Samos was captured by Athens from the Persians in 365 and retained until 322.

62.3 Reappointment was probably allowed to some of the (few) civilian offices filled by election also. Reappointment, like election, was appropriate when it was important that posts should be filled by the best men; a ban on reappointment, like appointment by lot, was appropriate for posts which did not need special ability but in which all could take their turn. Presumably two years in the council were allowed because otherwise the five hundred places could not be filled each year.

63.1 In chapters 63–9 the author uses 'archon' and '*thesmothetes*' indifferently to refer to any member of the board comprising the nine archons and the secretary to the *thesmothetae*.

63.2 Figure 2 (p. 159) indicates schematically the arrangements which are implied: it is presupposed that all the courts are together within a fenced-off area; a group of buildings, of the late fifth to mid fourth centuries, in the north-east of the Agora may have been used as a set of courts, but our other evidence does not suggest that all the courts formed a single complex in this way. The use of the equipment is explained in the sections that follow; probably by the time of the *Athenian Constitution* specially manufactured tokens were used as 'acorns'.

63.3 Jurors were registered each year: in the fifth century (24.3), and probably in the fourth also, the panel numbered six thousand. For 'indication' see 52.1: this is a special instance of the offence of exercising a right to which one was not entitled. For the imprisonment of men in debt to the state see 48.1.

63.4 No wooden tickets survive, but about two hundred tickets survive

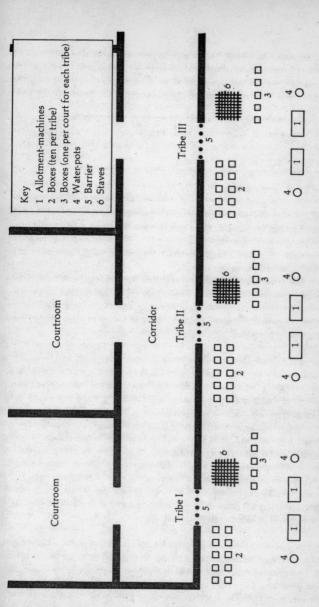

Figure 2   A schematic representation of the court complex

which are made of bronze but otherwise answer to the description of the wooden tickets: the one illustrated in figure 3 (below) bears on the left the section-letter *eta* and the design used on three-obol coins (indicating that the bearer has been registered for jury service), in the middle the bearer's

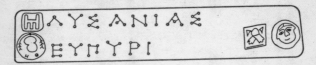

Figure 3   A juror's ticket

name (Lysanias of Eupyridae; the father's name is omitted), and on the right a special stamp (perhaps used to validate the tickets of a particular year) and a gorgon's-head stamp (indicating that the bearer was eligible for appointment to public office, to which the use of tickets and allotment-machines was in due course extended).

63.5 The letters *alpha* to *kappa* are used for the sections of the tribes; to avoid confusion, letters from *lambda* onwards (see section 2) are used to designate courts. The daily allotment of letters to courtrooms is an unnecessary refinement: random assignment of jurors to lawsuits could be achieved as well without it.

64.2–3 A pair of allotment-machines is illustrated in figure 4 (p. 161). Each machine has a tube with an open funnel at the top and a release mechanism at the bottom. If the first cube released is white, the five men whose tickets have been placed in the top row are selected to serve; if the second is black, the five men whose tickets have been placed in the second row are rejected; and so on until all the white cubes have been released and the required number of jurors has been selected. There will normally be more tickets in some columns than in others: there will be as many cubes as there are tickets in the shortest column, and men whose tickets are placed lower than the last ticket in the shortest column will have no chance of being selected.

64.4–5 The allotment-machines select the jurors; the drawing of an acorn assigns each selected juror to his court. The juror deposits his ticket in a box which will be taken to his court (65.4).

65.1–2 The use of both a letter and a colour to designate a courtroom is an unnecessary refinement, and creates the risk of an error by the attendant. There is no further mention of the 'official token' (possibly it assigned the recipient to a seat in his courtroom), and no explanation of the official who issues it.

65.3 'Retain their acorn and staff and take their seats in the court' has been inserted by editors to fill a lacuna: some prefer 'surrender their acorn and staff in the court' (cf. 68.2), but the reference to the staves in 69.2 makes the first version more likely even though it is procedurally less tidy.

65.4 For the five men who are to pay the jurors see 66.3.

66.1 It would have been simpler to have an allotment of officials only, giving court *lambda* to the first man drawn, *mu* to the second, and so on.

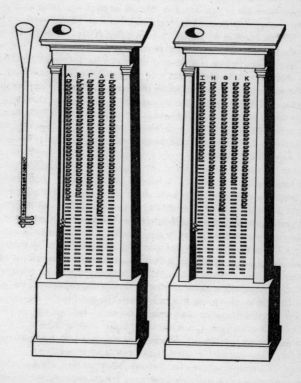

Figure 4   A pair of allotment-machines, for the selection of jurors

Since any presiding official might be combined with any jury, we must conclude that only one size of jury was used, and therefore only one grade of lawsuit was tried, each day. However, major public lawsuits with large juries were presumably not very numerous, and this would mean that prediction and bribery of the jurors would be easiest in the most important cases; so probably this conclusion should be modified to allow one major public suit with a jury of 1,001 or more (68.1) to be tried on the same day as lesser public suits with juries of 501.

67.1 The four categories are those of section 2; we may doubt whether there often occurred equal numbers of suits in the four categories, and should perhaps see four as the maximum number of cases which one court could be required to try in one day. For 'four in number, one from each' some editors prefer 'four in number from each', but there would not have been time for one court to try sixteen cases in a day. It appears that every trial, even the major public trials, had to be completed within a day.

67.2–3 A water-clock is illustrated in figure 5 (p. 163): each bowl has a hole near the rim, to ensure that it is always filled to the same level, and a tube at the bottom through which the water flows out; it empties in six minutes, and X X indicates that its capacity is two measures (*choes*). The bowls shown will not have been used in the courts, since they bear the name of a tribe, Antiochis. If the clock was to be stopped, for business which did not count against the speaker's time allowance, the tube had to be blocked. The allowances of section 2 apply to private suits: according to the sum at issue these might have juries of 201 or 401 (53.3), and probably what is said here applies to the larger cases only; for that reason 2,000 drachmae has been restored as the upper limit of the third category (but some editors restore 1,000 drachmae). 'Adjudications' are of claims, to an inheritance, for example, to which there may be more than two parties. In the first sentence of section 3 some editors restore 'a decree or law or testimony or agreement'.

67.4 The measured-out day was used for public suits: the allowances were based on the length of the day in Posideon, the month in which the winter solstice fell, and therefore did not fill the whole day at other times of the year. Other evidence suggests that in the time of the *Athenian Constitution* four jars (of thirty-six minutes each) were allowed for the plaintiff, four for the defendant, and in cases which required it three for the speeches of both on the assessment; earlier there had been a simple division of the day into three parts for plaintiff, defendant and voting; perhaps it was earlier still that the allowance for the two litigants was not subdivided.

67.5 The reconstruction of the second sentence may not be right; the measured-out day should have been used for all public suits, but not all involved an assessment.

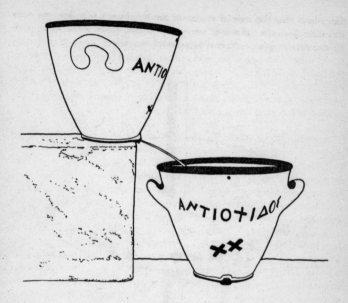

Figure 5   A water-clock

68.1 *Heliaea* normally refers to Solon's appeal court (see on 9.1), or to a jury-court, regarded as a subdivision of that; but the word was used also of the largest courtroom. We do not know how the size of jury for a public suit was decided (and chapters 63–5 do not explain how the odd one juror above the round hundred was appointed).

68.2 A juror's ballot is illustrated in figure 6 (p. 164; the inscription means 'official ballot'). Each juror had one with a hollow axle and one with a solid axle, and if he held them with his fingers and thumbs over the ends of the axles (section 4) he could feel, but no one could see, which ballot was which. For the men in charge of the ballots see 66.2; for 'the man appointed by lot for this task' see 65.2. For 'the staves' those who prefer the alternative reconstruction of 65.3 restore 'the tokens'.

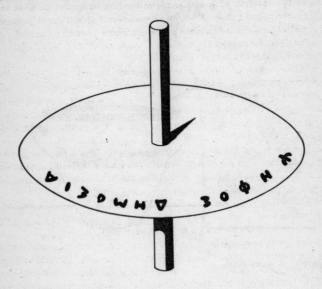

Figure 6   A juror's ballot

69.1 Since there was an odd number of jurors, and each juror had to vote to earn his pay, tied votes should not have occurred: perhaps the rule was a survival from times when the courts were less efficiently organized, and in the late fourth century was retained but was only exceptionally needed (for instance, if a juror was taken ill during the day).

69.2 For the divisions to which the jurors are assigned see 66.3. The short time allowance for the assessment will have applied not in public suits (67.4–5) but only in private.

The Epitome of Heraclides

1 For Athens under the kings see pp. 39–40. This is the most important part of the *Epitome*, as it and 41.2 give the best indication of what was in the lost beginning of the *Athenian Constitution*. Pandion's sons 'persisted in strife', but it was the Athenians as a whole whom Theseus reconciled.

2 For Cylon see chapter 1.

3 For Solon see chapters 5–12.

4 For the tyranny of Pisistratus and his sons see chapters 14–19; Harmodius and Aristogiton failed to kill Hippias but succeeded in killing Hipparchus, and then Hippias's rule became bitter. It was Cleisthenes who introduced the law about ostracism, for which see chapter 22.

5 It was not Ephialtes (chapter 25) but Cimon (chapters 26–7) who made generous use of his estates.

6 For Cleon and his successors see chapter 28. It was the Thirty who eliminated fifteen hundred men; Thrasybulus led the returning democrats, while Rhinon was a member of the Ten but prominent in the restored democracy (chapters 34–40).

7 Themistocles and Aristides should have been mentioned not here but between sections 4 and 5: they are mentioned as partners in 23.3; and for the dominance of the Areopagus see 23.1 and 25.1.

8 Preventing obstruction of the streets was one of the responsibilities of the city magistrates (50.2). The Eleven are treated in 52.1. The nine archons are treated in chapters 55–9: the fact that six of the nine are *thesmothetae*, and the scrutiny and oath, in chapter 55; the *basileus* in chapter 57; it was the polemarch who had military responsibilities, by the fourth century limited to religious observances, and he is treated in chapter 58.

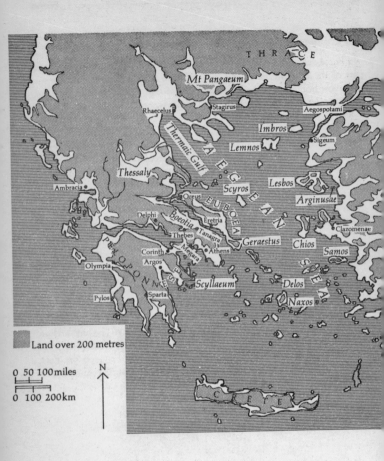

THRACE

Mt Pangaeum

Rhaecelus
Stagirus
Aegospotami

Imbros

Thermaic Gulf
Sigeum

Lemnos

Thessaly

Ambracia

Scyros
Lesbos

Arginusae

Oreus
Delphi
Boeotia
Eretria
EUBOEA
Clazomenae

Thebes
Tanagra
Geraestus
Chios

Corinth
Megara
Athens

Olympia
PELOPONNESE
Argos
Samos

Scyllaeum
Delos

Sparta
Pylos
Naxos

AEGEAN SEA

■ Land over 200 metres

0 50 100 miles
0 100 200 km

N

CRETE

Map 1 | Greece

Map 2 | Attica

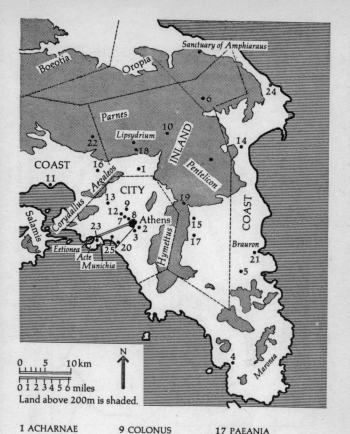

Demes are located by numbers (for Coele, Collytus, Cydathenaeum, Melite and Scambonidae, inside the city walls, see map 3), and the names of Cleisthenes' three regions are given in large capitals and mountains in large italics. Regional boundaries are purely schematic.

Map 3   Athens

Names of demes are in capital letters; principal modern streets are shown in pecked lines

Key to Map 3

1 Brauronian Artemis, sanctuary of
2 Council-house, new
3 Council-house, old
4 Delphinian Apollo, temple of
5 Delphinium, court at the
6 Eleusinium
7 Erechtheum
8 Gaol
9 Heliaea (?)
10 Hephaestus, temple of (commonly, but wrongly, called Theseum)
11 Lawcourts
12 Leocoreum
13 Odeum
14 Olympian Zeus, temple of
15 Palladium, court at the
16 Parthenon
17 Portico of the Basileus
18 Propylaea
19 Round House
20 South Portico
21 Strategeum (generals' office)
22 Theatre of Dionysus
23 Tribal heroes, statues of

CHRONOLOGICAL TABLE

683/2	Date claimed for first annual archon
630s–620s	Attempted coup of Cylon
621/0	Legislation of Draco
594/3	Archonship and reforms of Solon
561/0	First coup of Pisistratus
546/5–511/0	Tyranny of Pisistratus and sons
528/7	Death of Pisistratus
514/3	Murder of Hipparchus
511/0	Expulsion of Hippias
508/7	Reforms of Cleisthenes
490	First Persian invasion (battle of Marathon)
480–479	Second Persian invasion (battle of Salamis, 480)
462/1	Reforms of Ephialtes
431–404	Peloponnesian War
411	Oligarchy of Four Hundred
411/0	Intermediate regime
404–403	Oligarchy of Thirty and Ten
332–322	*Athenian Constitution* written and revised

BIBLIOGRAPHY

1. GREEK TEXT

The most easily accessible editions are:

F. G. Kenyon (ed.), *Aristotelis Atheniensium Respublica* (Oxford Classical Texts), Oxford University Press, 1920

H. Oppermann (ed.), *Aristotelis Athenaion Politeia*, Leipzig: Teubner, 1928; reprints with revised bibliography Stuttgart: Teubner, 1961 and subsequently. To be replaced by a new edition by M. H. Chambers.

The reconstruction of 67.4–68.1 which I translate is to be found in: H. Hommel, *Heliaia* (*Philologus*, Supplement 19.2), Leipzig: Dieterich, 1927

The text of the *Epitome of Heraclides* which I translate is to be found in: M. R. Dilts (ed.), *Heraclidis Lembi Excerpta Politiarum* (*Greek, Roman and Byzantine Monographs*, 5), Durham, North Carolina: Duke University, 1971

2. BOOKS ABOUT ARISTOTLE AND THE ATHENIAN CONSTITUTION

J. H. Day and M. H. Chambers, *Aristotle's History of Athenian Democracy* (University of California Publications in History, 73), University of California Press, 1962

G. Kaibel, *Stil und Text der Politeia Athenaion des Aristoteles*, Berlin: Weidmann, 1893

J. P. Lynch, *Aristotle's School: A Study of a Greek Educational Institution*, University of California Press, 1972

G. Mathieu, *Aristote, Constitution d'Athènes: essai sur la méthode suivie par Aristote dans la discussion des textes* (Bibliothèque de l'École des Hautes Études, 216), Paris: Champion, 1915

P. J. Rhodes, *A Commentary on the Aristotelian Athenaion Politeìa*, Oxford University Press, 1981

J. H. Schreiner, *Aristotle and Perikles: A Study in Historiography* (*Symbolae Osloenses*, Supplement 21), Oslo University Press, 1968

Bibliography

R. Weil, *Aristote et l'histoire: essai sur la Politique*, Paris: Klincksieck, 1960

U. von Wilamowitz-Moellendorff, *Aristoteles und Athen*, Berlin: Weidmann, 1893

3. BOOKS IN ENGLISH ABOUT POLITICAL INSTITUTIONS

V. L. Ehrenberg, *The Greek State* (2nd English edition), Methuen (USA: Barnes and Noble), 1969

W. G. Forrest, *The Emergence of Greek Democracy: The Character of Greek Politics, 800–400 B.C.*, Weidenfeld and Nicolson (USA: McGraw-Hill), 1966

G. Gilbert (trans. E. J. Brooks and T. Nicklin), *The Constitutional Antiquities of Sparta and Athens*, Sonnenschein (USA: Macmillan), 1895

G. Glotz (trans. N. Mallinson), *The Greek City and its Institutions*, Routledge (USA: Knopf), 1929

A. R. W. Harrison, *The Law of Athens*, Oxford University Press, 1968/71

C. Hignett, *A History of the Athenian Constitution to the End of the Fifth Century B.C.*, Oxford University Press, 1952

A. H. M. Jones, *Athenian Democracy*, Blackwell (USA: Praeger), 1957

D. M. MacDowell, *The Law in Classical Athens*, Thames and Hudson (USA: Cornell University Press), 1978

E. S. Staveley, *Greek and Roman Voting and Elections*, Thames and Hudson (USA: Cornell University Press), 1972

4. OTHER ANCIENT TEXTS CITED

I list below those ancient texts to which specific references are given in this book: there are Loeb editions, with original text and English translation on facing pages, of all except Justin; there are Penguin Classics translations of those marked with an asterisk.

Andocides, 5th–4th centuries BC, orator. *On the Mysteries* (Loeb *Minor Attic Orators*, i; *Greek Political Oratory*)

Antiphon, 5th century BC, orator. *On the Murder of Herodes* (Loeb *Minor Attic Orators*, i)

Aristophanes, 5th–4th centuries BC, comic dramatist. *Wasps**

Aristotle, 4th century BC, philosopher. *Movements of Animals*; *Nicomachean Ethics**; *Physics*; *Poetics* (*Classical Literary Criticism*); *Politics**; *Rhetoric*

Demosthenes, 4th century BC, orator. *Against Aristocrates*; *Against Macartatus* (preserved with works of Demosthenes, but not by him); *Against Timocrates*

Diodorus of Sicily, 1st century BC, historian

Herodotus, 5th century BC, historian*

Justin, 3rd century AD, epitome of history by Pompeius Trogus (1st century BC, in Latin)

Lysias, 5th–4th centuries BC, orator. *Against Eratosthenes* (*Greek Political Oratory*)

Plutarch, 1st–2nd centuries AD, *inter alia* biographer. *Cimon*; *Pericles*; *Solon*; *Themistocles* (all in *The Rise and Fall of Athens*)

Thucydides, 5th century BC, historian*

Xenophon, 5th–4th centuries BC, *inter alia* historian. *Hellenica* (*A History of My Times*)

Androtion, 4th century BC, author of an *Atthis* (history of Athens: see p. 19). All that survive are 'fragments' quoted by later writers. The most important fragments dealing with the fifth and earlier centuries are translated in C. W. Fornara, *Archaic Times to the End of the Peloponnesian War* (*Translated Documents of Greece and Rome*, Vol. I), Johns Hopkins University Press, 1977; 2nd edition, Cambridge University Press, 1983

GLOSSARY AND SUBJECT INDEX

Calendar

Each Greek city had its own system of identifying years, and its own calendar. In Athens the year was identified by the name of the archon; the year began in midsummer, so the year of Solon's archonship was 594/3 BC, that is, summer 594–summer 593. The Athenian months were:

1. Hecatombaeon	5. Maemacterion	9. Elaphebolion
2. Metageitnion	6. Posideon	10. Munychion
3. Boedromion	7. Gamelion	11. Thargelion
4. Pyanopsion	8. Anthesterion	12. Scirophorion

Hecatombaeon corresponded roughly to July, and so on. These were lunar months (see 43.2); from time to time an extra month had to be inserted, usually a second Posideon after the first, to keep the calendar in step with the seasons. Since some years contained twelve months and some thirteen, interest was always reckoned by the month, not by the year.

Measures, Weights, Coinage

Again each city had its own standards. The following Athenian units are used in this book (all modern equivalents are approximate):

Distance

1 stade = 193 yards = 176 metres

Capacity

	1 *kotyle*	= ½ imperial pint	= 285cc (wet or dry)
12 *kotylai*	= 1 *chous*	= 5¾ imperial pints	= 3.4 litres (wet)
12 *choes*	= 1 *metretes*	= 9 imperial gallons	= 41 litres (wet)
192 *kotylai*	= 1 *medimnos*	= 11½ imperial gallons	= 55 litres (dry)

In 60.2 *kotyle* is translated 'cup'; in 67.2 *chous* is translated 'measure', and in

67.4 a 'jar' probably contained 1 *metretes*; in 7–8, 26.2 and 47.1 *medimnos* is translated 'bushel', and in 7.4 'measures' of dry and wet goods are *medimnoi* and *metretai* respectively.

Weights, coinage

6 obols	=	1 drachma
100 drachmae	=	1 mina
2 minas	=	1 stater
30 staters	=	1 talent

These were originally the names of weights, and after the introduction of coinage they came to be applied to the values represented by those weights of silver. Chapter 10 alleges, probably wrongly, that before the reforms of Solon Athens divided its mina into 70 drachmae. The Athenian mina weight was about 14 oz. (390 g) in the late sixth century, about 16 oz. (460 g) in the late fifth and fourth centuries; throughout this period the weight of 1 mina's worth of coins remained steady at 15 oz. (430 g).

Direct translation of ancient into modern currency is impossible, but the following examples will give an idea of the value of money. In the late fifth century an unskilled worker could earn ½ drachma a day and a skilled 1 drachma; in the late fourth an unskilled worker could earn 1½ drachmae and a skilled 2–2½ drachmae. In the fourth century an invalid was entitled to a maintenance grant if his property was less than 3 minas; a man would be liable to such burdens as the trierarchy if his property was more than about 4 talents; one of the largest fifth-century estates is said to have been 200 talents, but there cannot have been many estates which exceeded a tenth of that figure. The total annual revenue of Athens was about 1,000 talents in 431 (including the tribute paid by the member states of the Delian League), and increased from 130 to 400 talents between 355 and 341.

Glossary

In the alphabetical list which follows, technical terms are given both in Greek and in translation, and explanations and references are given against the form of the term which is used in the text. The spelling of Greek words and names in English is a controversial matter on which agreement is unlikely ever to be achieved: as far as possible, all names, and words which I have used in the text, are given in anglicized or latinized form (for example, Aristotle, polemarch, *colacretae*), but words which are used not in the text but only in the Notes and in this Glossary are directly transliterated (for example, *katalogeis*). I have not indexed every appearance of every term: there would be little value, for instance, in a complete list of references to tribes. Except where otherwise stated, references are to chapters and sections of the *Athenian Constitution; Epit.* denotes the *Epitome of Heraclides.*

Acorn (*balanos*): *see* Token.

Acropolis. Citadel on which the principal temples stood (map 3): p. 41, 14.1, 19.6, 20.3, 37.2, 55.5, 60.3.

Adjudication (*diadikasia*): of rival claims to enjoy some benefit or to avoid some burden, 56.6, 57.2, 67.2; of claims to exemption from the trierarchy, 61.1.

Advocates (*synegoroi*). Assistants of the auditors: 54.2.

Adynatoi: *see* Invalids.

Agora (market). The main square of Athens (map 3): 38.1, 52.2, 57.4.

Agoranomoi: *see* Market magistrates.

Agroikoi: *see* Farmers.

Allocation (*merismos*). Distribution of public revenue among the various spending authorities: 48.2.

Allotment-machine (*kleroterion*): 63.1, 64.2–3, 66.1; see figure 4.

Ammonias. Ship used on formal state business, replacing a ship called *Salaminia c.*350 (cf. *Paralus*): 61.7.

Amphiaraus. Hero; Amphiarea possibly mentioned in 54.7: 54.7n.

Amphictyons (neighbours). Officials with financial responsibility for the sanctuary of Apollo on Delos: 62.2; *see also* Sacred recorder.

Antidosis: *see* Challenge to exchange.

Apagoge: *see* Delivery.

Apodektai: *see* Receivers.

Apollo. God: archons required to have cult of, 55.3; *see also* Pilgrimage, Thargelia; *and* Delos, Delphi, Delphinium, in Index of Persons and Places.

Apotimema: *see* Valuation.

Appeal: *see* Reference.

Arbitrators (*diaitetai*). Men in their last year on the military registers, commissioned to decide private lawsuits: 53.2–6.

Architheoros: *see* Pilgrimage.

Archon (ruler). Official created to take over some of the powers of the king; in broader sense, any member of a board of nine officials of whom the archon was one: pp. 39–40, 3, 55–9, *Epit.* 8; cf. 8.1–2, 22.5, 26.2, 29.5, 30.5, 62.2. In a still broader sense, the Greek word can be used of any official: it is used of the governor of Salamis, 54.8, 62.2.

Areopagus. Hill west of the Acropolis (map 3). Name given to council of

Cadets (*epheboi*). Ancient name for men newly come of age; used of Athenians performing national service for two years after coming of age: 42.2–5; cf. 53.4.

Cavalry (*hippeis*): 24.3, 38.2, 49.1–2, 61.4–6; the second of Solon's four property-classes: 7.3–4; cf. 4.3, 26.2.

Cavalry commanders (*hipparchoi*). Commanders in chief of the cavalry: 4.2, 30.2, 31.3, 44.4, 61.4; cavalry commander for Lemnos, 61.6.

Chairman (*epistates*): of the prytany or the presiding committee, 44, 59.2.

Challenge to exchange (*antidosis*). If a man designated to perform a liturgy thought that a man who had been passed over was richer than himself and not exempt, he could challenge the other man either to perform the liturgy or to show that he was not richer by exchanging property: 56.2, 61.1.

Choregus. Rich citizen performing the liturgy of taking general and financial responsibility for a chorus participating in a festival: 54.8, 56.2; *choregia* metaphorical, translated 'service', 27.4.

City magistrates (*astynomoi*): 50.2, *Epit*. 8.

Civic rights, loss of (later significance of *atimia*): 53.5, 63.3, 67.5; cf. 16.10, where author misunderstands outlawry.

Claim to exemption (*skepsis*): from performance of a liturgy, 56.2.

Clan (*genos*). A group of families, supposedly or actually related: an aristocracy, but wider than that of the Well-born, p. 40, 21.6, 57.2.

Club (*hetaireia*). An association of citizens, often formed with a view to collaboration in public life; used by the extreme oligarchs of 404: 34.3. (In 20.1 *hetaireiai* is translated as 'party struggle': the author is paraphrasing Herodotus, and does not imply that such clubs existed in 508/7.)

Colacretae (ham-collectors). Paying officers of the Athenian treasury, until 411 or shortly before: 7.3, 30.2n.

Commissioners (*probouloi*). A board of ten appointed after Athens' failure in Sicily in 413, to take over some of the functions of the council: 29.2.

Company commanders (*lochagoi*). Commanders of companies (*lochoi*) within the tribal regiments of hoplites: 61.3; the cadets had their own company commanders.

Complaint (*probole*). A plea that a man had been wronged, on which the assembly voted, after which orthodox judicial proceedings might but need not follow: 43.5, 59.2.

Corn-guardians (*sitophylakes*): 51.3.

Cosmetes (one who makes orderly). Supervisor in chief of the cadets: 42.2.

Council (*boule*). Body which prepared business for the assembly and, in the fifth and fourth centuries, coordinated the administration of the state: 4.3, 8.4, 43.9; cf. 21.3, 24.3, 25.2, 30–32, 37.1, 62.2; *see also* Areopagus.

Council-house (*bouleuterion*) (map 3): 32.3, 48.1–2, 53.4.

Decree (*psephisma*). Resolution taken by vote, especially in the council and assembly. In the fourth century Athens distinguished between (superior) laws, enacted by a special procedure (see p. 89), and (inferior) decrees, and this distinction underlies what is said of laws in 26.2 and of decrees in 41.2.

Delian League. Modern name for the alliance made by Athens to continue fighting against Persia after the war against Xerxes, which Athens came increasingly to treat as an empire, and which Sparta destroyed by defeating Athens in the Peloponnesian War: 23.4–24; cf. 27.1, 32.3, 41.2.

Delivery (*apagoge*). Procedure available against certain kinds of offender, by which any citizen might hale the offender before the authorities: 52.1; cf. 29.4.

Demarch. Chief officer of deme: 21.5, 54.8.

Deme (*demos*, in the sense of local community). Name used of the 139 units into which Cleisthenes divided Attica: 21.4–5; cf. 42.1, 55.3, 62.1. The Greek word can also denote 'people', either the whole community (and, as a special sense of that, the assembly of the citizens) or the poor and unprivileged as opposed to the rich and powerful.

Deme justices. Magistrates who visited the demes to decide minor private lawsuits: 16.5, 26.3. In the fourth century they ceased to visit the demes and became known as the forty, but the old title is used in 48.5.

Demeter. Goddess: *see* Eleusinia, Mysteries, Sacred recorder.

Demiourgoi: *see* Workers for the People.

Denunciation (*eisangelia*): of major offences against the state, 8.4, 29.4, 43.4, 59.2, perhaps 4.4; of offences committed by officials, 45.2, perhaps 4.4; of offences committed by arbitrators, 53.6. The term is also used, though not in the *Athenian Constitution*, of the first four lawsuits listed in 56.6.

Dependants (*pelatai*). Term used as equivalent of 'sixth-parters': 2.2.

Deposit (*parastasis*). Demanded from prosecutor in certain lawsuits: 59.3.

Diadikasia: *see* Adjudication.

Diaitetai: *see* Arbitrators.

Dikai: *see* Lawsuits.

Dikasteria: *see* Jury-courts.

Dionysus. God: sacred marriage with *basileus*' wife, 3.5; Great Dionysia, 56.3–5; Dionysia at the Lenaeum (usually called the Lenaea), 57.1; Dionysia in Piraeus and Salamis, 54.8; theatre of Dionysus (map 3) used for cadets' display, 42.4.

Dokimasia: *see* Scrutiny.

Eisagogeis: *see* Introducers.

Eisangelia: *see* Denunciation.

Ekklesia: *see* Assembly.

Eleusinia. Festival of the goddesses Demeter and Persephone of Eleusis: 54.7; *see also* Mysteries.

Eleven. Gaolers and executioners: 52.1, *Epit.* 8; cf. 7.3, 24.3, 29.4, 35.1, 39.6.

Empektes: *see* Inserter.

Emporion: *see* Overseers.

Enagismata: *see* Heroes.

Endeixis: *see* Indication.

Enyalius. God: sacrifice to, 58.1.

Epheboi: *see* Cadets.

Ephesis: *see* Reference.

Epibole: *see* Summary fine.

Epicheirotonia: *see* Vote of confidence.

Epikleros: *see* Heiress.

Epimeletai: *see* Overseers.

Epistates: *see* Chairman.

Equal obligations, man of (*isoteles*). A free non-citizen temporarily or permanently resident in Athens, granted the privilege of equality with Athenian citizens in certain respects: 58.2.

Eupatridai: *see* Well-born.

Euthynai, Euthynoi: *see* Examination.

Examination (*euthynai*). Inquiry into a man's conduct in office, after his retirement; the word is used properly of the more general inquiry, but can be used also of the audit of his accounts (for which see Auditors); any citizen might lodge a charge with the examiners (*euthynoi*): 48.4–5; cf. 4.2, 27.1, 38.4, 39.5, 56.1, 59.2.

Exchange: *see* Challenge, Overseers.

Farmers (*georgoi*). One of the two classes said to have been created by Ion: pp. 39–40; given derogatory name 'rustics' (*agroikoi*), 13.2; *see also* Workers for the People.

Festival fund (theoric fund). Fund set up to make grants to citizens to cover the cost of theatre tickets at major festivals, used for other purposes also as money accumulated: 43.1, 47.2.

Five-hundred-bushel class (*pentakosiomedimnoi*). The highest of Solon's four property-classes: 7.3–8.1; cf. 4.3, 26.2, 47.1.

Five Thousand. Body supposed to have full political rights 411–410: 29–33; cf. p. 78, 41.2n.

Forty. Title given in the fourth century to the officials formerly known as deme justices, involved in the trial of private lawsuits: 53.1–5; cf. 48.5, 58.2.

Four Hundred. Oligarchic council of 411: 29–33; cf. p. 78, 41.2; cf. Solon's council of four hundred, 8.4; also council of 401 in 'Constitution of Draco', 4.3.

Garrison commander (harmost). Spartan official sent to Athens 404–403: 37.2.

Generals (*strategoi*). Commanders-in-chief of the armed forces: 22.2, 61.1–2; cf. 4.2, 30.2, 31.2–3, 44.4.

Genos: see Clan.

Georgoi: see Farmers.

Governor of Salamis: *see* Archon.

Grammateus: see Secretary.

Graphai: see Lawsuits.

Hamippi (those with the horses). A body of light-armed cavalry who fought with the regular cavalry: 49.1.

Harmost: *see* Garrison commander.

Heiress (*epikleros*). The daughter of a man with no legitimate sons; at his death, unless previously or by will married to a man whom the father adopted as his son, was to be married to her nearest male kin so that the property, in descending to her sons, should remain within the family: 9.2, 43.4, 56.6–7, 58.3.

Hektemoroi: see Sixth-parters.

Heliaea. Name given, but not in the *Athenian Constitution*, to Solon's appeal court: 9.1, p. 28; the largest court building (possible location, map 3), 68.1.

Hellenotamiae (Greek treasurers). Treasurers of the Delian League, in or before 411 given responsibility for the funds of the Athenian state also: 30.2; ceased to exist with the League at the end of the Peloponnesian War.

Hephaestus. God; Hephaestia doubtful reading in 54.7.

Heracles. Hero; Heraclea; 54.7.

Heroes: of Cleisthenes' ten tribes, 21.6, 48.4, 53.4; of the forty-two year-classes: 53.4–7; heroes' rites (*enagismata*), distinct from the rites of the gods, for Harmodius and Aristogiton: 58.1; *see also* Amphiaraus, Heracles.

Hetaireia: see Club.

Hieromnemon: see Sacred recorder.

Hieron episkeuastai: see Repairers of temples.

Hieropoei (doers of sacred things). Boards of men similar to priests, responsible for certain religious ceremonies: 30.2, 54.6–7.

Hiketeria: see Supplication.

Hipparchoi: see Cavalry commanders.

Hippeis: see Cavalry.

Hodopoioi: see Roadbuilders.

Hoplites. Heavy infantry: 4.2, 24.3, 33.1–2, 61.1; *see also* Rankers.

Illegal proposal, prosecution for (*graphe paranomon*). Charge of illegally proposing a decree in the council or assembly, in fact used against decrees whether charged with being illegal or inexpedient (contrast Inexpedient law), to annul the decree and (if charge made within a year) penalize proposer: 29.4, 45.4, 59.2.

Indication (*endeixis*). Procedure available against certain kinds of offender, by which any citizen might point out the offender to the authorities: 52.1; cf. 29.4, 63.3.

Inexpedient law, prosecution for enacting (*graphe nomon me epitedeion theinai*). Charge of proposing an inexpedient law, in fact used against laws whether charged with being illegal or inexpedient (contrast Illegal proposal), to annul the law and (if charge made within a year) penalize proposer: 59.2.

Inserter (*empektes*). Man who inserted jurors' tickets in allotment-machines: 64.2–3.

Introducers (*eisagogeis*). Used in general of any officials who presided in a jury-court; in particular of those responsible for certain 'monthly' lawsuits: 52.2–3.

Invalids (*adynatoi*). Men unable to earn a living and with little property, paid a maintenance grant by the state: 49.4.

Isoteles: *see* Equal obligations.

Judicial agreement (*symbolon*). With another city, on procedure to be followed in lawsuits between an Athenian and a citizen of that city: 59.6.

Jury-courts (*dikasteria*): 63–9; cf. 7.3, 9, 24.3, 25.2, 27.3–5, 45.1–3, 52.1, 53.3, 59, 62.2.

Katalogeis: *see* Registrars.

King: *see* Basileus.

Kleroterion: *see* Allotment-machine.

Kyrbeis. Name of unknown meaning given to the monuments on which Draco's and Solon's laws were inscribed: 7.1; also, though not in the *Athenian Constitution*, known as *axones* (axles). See figure 1.

Labourers (*thetes*). The lowest of Solon's four property-classes: 7.3–4.

Law (*nomos*). Used of the enactments of Draco, 41.2; of Solon, 6.1, 7.1–2, 22.1, *Epit.* 3; of Cleisthenes, 22.1, 29.3; of Ephialtes, 35.2; *see also* Decree, Ordinance.

Lawsuits, categories of: public suits (*graphai*), on charges on which any citizen might prosecute, contrasted with private suits (*dikai*), on charges on which only the injured party or his kin might prosecute, 9.1, 53, 67–68.1;

assessed suits, where prosecutor and defendant each submitted an assessment of the appropriate penalty or damages and, if the defendant was found guilty, the court had to choose between the two, contrasted with unassessed suits, where a fixed penalty was laid down by law: *see* Assessment. For special procedures *see* Adjudication, Arbitrators, Areopagus, Auditors, Challenge to exchange, Claim to exemption, Complaint, Delivery, Deme justices, Denunciation, Examination, Forty, Illegal proposal, Indication, Inexpedient law, Introducers, Reference, Scrutiny, Summary fine.

Lenaea: *see* Dionysus.

Liturgy. A public duty, involving responsibility for and the expenditure of one's private funds on a set of performers at a festival (*see Choregus*) or a ship in the navy (*see* Trierarch), imposed on a rich citizen: 27.3, 56.3.

Lochagoi: *see* Company commanders.

Logistai: *see* Auditors.

Malicious prosecutors (*sykophantai*). Men who for their own advantage exploited the opportunity provided for any citizen to prosecute in public lawsuits (*see* Lawsuits): 35.2–3, 43.5, 59.3.

Market magistrates (*agoranomoi*): 51.1.

Measures magistrates (*metronomoi*): 51.2.

Merismos: *see* Allocation.

Metic (immigrant). A free non-citizen, registered as a temporary or permanent resident in Athens, and consequently given certain rights at law and certain obligations in respect of taxes and military service: 43.5, 57.3, 58.2–3. For privileged categories of metic *see* Equal obligations, Proxenus.

Metronomoi: *see* Measures magistrates.

Mysteries. Of the goddesses Demeter and Persephone of Eleusis: 57.1; cf. 39.2, 56.4.

Naucrariae. Organizations in early Athens, headed by officials called *naucrari*, which were probably responsible for providing ships for the navy; little is known about them, and they were abolished either by Cleisthenes or early in the fifth century (*see* 21.5n.): 8.3, 21.5.

Nomon me epitedeion theinai, graphe: *see* Inexpedient law.

Nomos: *see* Law.

Ordinance (*thesmos*): used of the enactments of Draco, 4.1, 7.1; of Solon, 12.4, 35.2.

Ostracism (potsherding). A device by which the assembly could vote each year to send one man into honourable exile for ten years; there was no list of candidates, but each voter wrote the name of the man whom he wished to expel on a potsherd (*ostrakon*: several thousands have been found); ostracism remained theoretically available in the fourth century but was last used *c.* 416: 22, 43.5, *Epit.* 4; cf. 27.4.

Outlawry (original significance of *atimia*): 8.5, 22.8; cf. 16.10, where author misunderstands it as denoting loss of civic rights.

Overseers (*epimeletai*): of the Dionysia, 56.4; of the dockyards, 46.1n.; of the exchange (*emporion*), 51.4; of the Mysteries, 57.1; unspecified, 30.2.

Panathenaea. Athenian national festival of Athena; one year in four, Great Panathenaea: 49.3, 54.7, 60, 62.2, cf. 18.2–3, 43.1.

Paralus. Ship used on formal state business (cf. *Ammonias*): 61.7.

Paranomon, graphe: see Illegal proposal.

Parastasis: see Deposit.

Paredroi: see Assistants.

Pelatai: see Dependants.

Pentakosiomedimnoi: see Five-hundred-bushel class.

Peplos: see Robe.

Persephone. Goddess, daughter of Demeter: *see* Eleusinia, Mysteries; *and* Persephone, in Index of Persons and Places.

Phratriai: see Brotherhoods.

Phylai: see Tribes.

Phylarchoi: see Squadron commanders.

Phylobasileis: see Tribes.

Pilgrimage (*theoria*). An official delegation to a festival at a sanctuary outside Attica; there was an annual pilgrimage to the sanctuary of Apollo on Delos, led by a pilgrim-leader (*architheoros*), with a particularly elaborate festival one year in four: 54.7, 56.3. The literal meaning of the Greek word is 'seeing', and it is translated 'to see the sights' in 11.1.

Pinakion: see Ticket.

Polemarch (war-leader). Official created to take over the military powers of the king; he in turn lost the military powers to the generals, and became simply one of the nine archons, with particular responsibility for metics: pp. 39–40, 3, 22.2, 58; title omitted, *Epit.* 8.

Polemarcheum (office of polemarch): 3.5.

Poletai: see Sellers.

Preliminary resolution (*probouleuma*). The resolution of the council which was needed to refer a matter to the assembly for debate; it could but did not have to embody a specific recommendation: 44.4, 45.4.

Preliminary vote (*procheirotonia*). In some circumstances the assembly held a preliminary vote, perhaps to decide which of the topics referred to it for debate it would consider, or in which order it would consider them; the *Athenian Constitution* states only that this is sometimes dispensed with: 43.6; and there is little other evidence.

Presiding committee (*proedroi*). Of the council and assembly: 44.2–3; cf. 59.2.

Principal Assembly (*kyria ekklesia*): 43.4, 62.2.

Probole: see Complaint.

Probouleuma: see Preliminary resolution.

Probouloi: see Commissioners.

Procheirotonia: see Preliminary vote.

Prodromi (advance-runners). A body of light-armed cavalry: 49.1.

Proedroi: see Presiding committee.

Proxenus. Originally a citizen of another state who lived in that state and was appointed by Athens to look after visiting Athenians; but such appointments became increasingly frequent and increasingly honorary, and could be used to confer a privileged status on metics who lived in Athens and might want to appear before Athenian courts: 54.3, 58.2.

Prytaneion: see Town hall.

Prytanes. A subdivision of the council consisting of the fifty members from one of Cleisthenes' ten tribes, who acted as standing committee and also, until the creation of a separate presiding committee, presided over meetings of the council and assembly; the word 'prytany' can refer either to a board of *prytanes* or to the period during which one board was in office: 43.3, 44; cf. 4.2, 29.4–5, 45.4, 62.2.

Psephisma: see Decree.

Rankers (*zeugitai*). Hoplites, as name of the third of Solon's property-classes: 7.3–4; cf. 4.3. 26.2.

Receivers (*apodektai*). Collectors of public revenue: 47.5–48.2, 52.3.

Reference (*ephesis*). Transfer of a lawsuit from one body to another, which has final authority, sometimes obligatory, sometimes on appeal by a litigant dissatisfied with the verdict of the first body: 9.1, 42.1, 45.1–3, 53.2–6, 55.2, 59.4.

Regimental commanders (*taxiarchoi*). Commanders of the tribal regiments of hoplites: 61.3; cf. 30.2, 31.3n.; the cadets had their own regimental commanders.

Registrars (*katalogeis*): of the cavalry, 49.2; of the Five Thousand in 411, 29.5; cf. register of the Three Thousand in 404–403, 36.

Repairers of temples (*hieron episkeuastai*): 50.1.

Roadbuilders (*hodopoioi*): 54.1.

Robe (*peplos*). The robe which was used to clothe the cult statue of Athena; 49.3, 60.1.

Round House (*tholos*). The headquarters of the *prytanes* (map 3): 43.3, 44.1.

Rustics: *see* Farmers.

Sacred recorder (*hieromnemon*). The voting representative sent by Athens to the Amphictyony, the body of Greek peoples responsible for the sanctuaries of Demeter at Anthela (near Thermopylae) and of Apollo at Delphi: 30.2.

Scrutiny (*dokimasia*). A formal check on a man's qualifications for citizenship, office, the invalid grant, etc.: 42.1–2, 45.3, 49, 55.2–4, 56.1, 59.4.

Secretary (*grammateus*): three principal state secretaries, 54.3–5; secretary to the *thesmothetae*, 55.1–2, 59.7, 63.1; secretary in a jury-court, 67.3.

Seisachtheia: see Shaking-off of Burdens.

Sellers (*poletai*). Makers of state contracts and sellers of confiscated property: 47.2–5; cf. 7.3.

Shaking-off of Burdens (*seisachtheia*). Name given to Solon's cancellation of debts: 8; cf. 12.4, *Epit.* 3, 56.2n.

Sitophylakes: see Corn-guardians.

Sixth-parters (*hektemoroi*). Dependent peasants who had to surrender a sixth of their produce to an overlord: 2.2; cf. 6.1n., 12.4n.

Skepsis: see Claim to exemption.

Sophronistae (those who make prudent). Supervisors of the tribal contingents of cadets: 42.2–3.

Squadron commanders (*phylarchoi*). Commanders of the tribal squadrons of cavalry: 61.5; cf. 30.2, 31.3.

Staff (*bakteria*): *see* Token.

Strategoi: see Generals.

Stratiotic fund: *see* Army fund.

Summary fine (*epibole*). A penalty which an official can impose on his own authority without reference to a jury-court: 56.7, 61.2; cf. 45.1n.

Supplication (*hiketeria*). The act of throwing oneself on the mercy of the gods: p. 41; secularized as a procedure by which a man asked something from the assembly not as his right but as a favour: 43.6.

Sykophantai: see Malicious prosecutors.

Symbolon: see Judicial agreement, Token.

Symmories. Groups of men liable for service as trierarchs; instituted *c.*357 (in imitation of the symmories instituted twenty years earlier to simplify the collection of the property tax called *eisphora*, 'paying in') as a mechanism through which those liable could make moderate payments every year instead of large payments in the years when their turn came round: 61.1.

Synegoroi: see Advocates.

Tamiai: see Treasurers.

Taxiarchoi: see Regimental commanders.

Ten: board replacing the Thirty in 403, and (an eccentricity of the *Athenian Constitution*) a second Ten replacing the first, 38; subsequent allusions, not mentioning a second Ten, 39.6, 41.2; ten governors of the Piraeus 404–403, 35.1, cf. 39.6. Most boards in democratic Athens were of ten men, one from each of Cleisthenes' tribes.

Thargelia. Festival of Apollo: 56.3–5.

Theatre: *see* Dionysus.

Theoria: see Pilgrimage.

Theoric fund: *see* Festival fund.

Thesmos: see Ordinance.

Thesmothetae (statute-setters). Six judicial officials who were added to the *basileus*, the archon and the polemarch to form the board of nine archons; subsequently given a secretary, so that the board comprised ten men and one could be appointed from each of Cleisthenes' tribes: 3, 55.1, 59, 63.1, *Epit.* 8; *thesmothetes* used of any member of the board of ten, 63.5, 64.1, 66.1.

Thesmotheteum (office of *thesmothetae*): 3.5.

Thetes: see Labourers.

Third (*trittys*). One third of a tribe, old or new: p. 40, 8.3, 21.3–4, 44.1.

Thirty. Ruling body of oligarchs 404–403: 34.2–41.1; cf. 41.2; number omitted, *Epit.* 6.

Tholos: see Round House.

Three Thousand. Body of privileged citizens 404–403: 36–7.

Ticket (*pinakion*). Issued to man registered for jury service, and used in conjunction with allotment-machines: 63.4; cf. 64, 65.3–4, 66.2. *See* figures 3 and 4.

Timema, Timesis: see Assessment.

Timetai: see Assessors.

Token (*symbolon*). Tokens issued to jurors: 65.2, 68.2n.; 68.2, 69.2; cf. the acorn (*balanos*), 63.2. 64.4, 65.1–3; and the staff (*bakteria*), 63.2, 65.1–3, 68.2, 69.2.

Town hall (*prytaneion*). The ceremonial headquarters of the state; originally the office of the archon, retained as the building containing the hearth where the city's sacred fire burned, and the building where those whom the state wished to honour were entertained: 3.5, 24.3, 62.2; Solon's laws perhaps preserved there from the fourth century, 7.1n.

Treasurers (*tamiai*): title used particularly of the treasurers of Athena, 4.2, 7.3, 8.1, 30.2, 47.1, 60.3; treasurers of the Other Gods, 30.2n., 47.1n.; treasurer of the council, 49.5; treasurers of the *Paralus* and *Ammonias*, 61.7; *see also* Army fund, *Colacretae*, Festival fund, *Hellenotamiae*.

Glossary and Subject Index

Tribes (*phylai*). Originally the citizens of Athens were divided into four tribes, based on actual or alleged kinship and allegedly named after the sons of Ion: pp. 39–40, 8.3, 41.2; divided into ten new tribes by Cleisthenes, based on the place of residence at that time but hereditary thereafter, 21, cf. 56.2, 62.1, 63.2, and many passages referring to appointments on a tribal basis; the old tribes remained in existence, and the four tribal heads (*phylobasileis*) retained a function in homicide trials, 21.2n., 57.4.

Trierarchs. Rich citizens accepting financial and general responsibility for a ship in the Athenian navy; originally one man appointed to one ship for a year, but from *c*.357 organized in symmories: 61.1.

Trieropoioi: *see* Trireme-builders.

Trireme-builders (*trieropoioi*). A sub-committee of the council: 46.1. On triremes and larger warships see 46.1n.

Trittys: *see* Third.

Tyrant. A man who usurps absolute power over the state: 1, 11.2, 12.3, 14–19, 20.4–5, 41.2, *Epit.* 2, *Epit.* 4; cf. 22.3–6, 27.3.

Valuation (*apotimema*). Of the security offered by a man wishing to lease an orphan's estate: 56.7.

Vote of confidence (*epicheirotonia*). A vote taken each prytany to decide whether the officials currently in office should continue in office: 43.4, 61.2, 4.

Well-born (*eupatridai*). A privileged group of aristocratic families, within the wider circle of the clans, said to have been set apart by Theseus but in fact the families which emerged most successful from the dark age following the breakdown of the Mycenaean civilization: pp. 39–40; cf. 2.2, 3.1, 3.6, 8.2, 20.3.

Workers for the People (*demiourgoi*). Word used often of craftsmen, in some states as title of officials; one of the two classes said to have been created by Ion: pp. 39–40, 13.2; *see also* Farmers.

Zeugitai: *see* Rankers.

Zeus. God: archons required to have cult of, 55.3; procession for Zeus the Saviour, 56.5; *see also* Palladium, in Index of Persons and Places.

INDEX OF PERSONS AND PLACES

Gods and heroes are included in this index for their legendary exploits, in the Glossary and Subject Index for their cult; buildings in Athens are included in this index if they have a proper name (for example, Bucoleum), in the Glossary and Subject Index if they have a common name (for example, town hall). Except where otherwise stated, references are to chapters and sections of the *Athenian Constitution*; *Epit.* denotes the *Epitome of Heraclides*.

Acastus. Legendary life archon, possibly but not certainly identical with the Acastus of the archons' oath: 3.3.

Acherdus. Deme: 38.3.

Acte. Part of Piraeus (map 2): garrisoned by cadets, 42.3; posting of a general, 61.1.

Aegeus. Legendary king of Athens: p. 39.

Aegospotami. Battle against Sparta 405/4 (map 1): 34.2.

Agyrrhius. Introduces and increases assembly pay after 403: 41.3.

Alcibiades. Important in the late fifth century but omitted from the *Athenian Constitution*: p. 73, 6.2–4n., 22.3–4n., 28.3n.

Alcmaeonids: cursed for killing Cylon's supporters, p. 41, 20.2–3; responsible for overthrow of Pisistratid tyranny, 19.3–4, 20.4–5; Cleisthenes an Alcmaeonid, 20.1–3, 28.2. The following other men mentioned in the *Athenian Constitution* were Alcmaeonids: Alcmeon, Cedon, Hippocrates, Megacles I, II, III; through his mother, Pericles; Cimon and Xanthippus married Alcmaeonids.

Alcmeon. Father of Megacles II, 13.4.

Alexias. Archon 405/4: 34.2.

Alopece. Deme (map 2): 22.5, 45.1.

Ambracia. Corinthian colony in north-west Greece (map 1): 17.4.

Anacreon. Lyric poet, invited to Athens by Hipparchus I: 18.1.

Anaphlystus. Deme (map 2): 29.1.

Anchimolus. Commander of first Spartan expedition against Hippias: 19.5.

Angele. Deme (map 2): 34.1.

Index of Persons and Places

Anthemion. Man who rose from labourers' to cavalry class and dedicated statue on Acropolis: 7.4; possibly father of Anytus.

Antidotus. Archon 451/0: 26.4.

Antiphon. Leading oligarch 411: 32.1; possible source of the *Athenian Constitution* on 411, p. 72.

Anytus: said to have bribed a jury *c*.409, 27.5; said to be supporter of Theramenes 404, 34.3; but with Thrasybulus at Phyle; one of Socrates' prosecutors 399; *see also* Anthemion.

Aphidna. Deme (map 2): 34.3.

Archestratus. Probably associate of Ephialtes; author of laws against Areopagus: 35.2.

Archinus I. Of Ambracia; first husband of Timonassa: 17.4.

Archinus II: said to be supporter of Theramenes 404, 34.3; but with Thrasybulus at Phyle,; upholder of moderation 403, 40.1–2.

Arginusae. Aegean islands (map 1); battle against Sparta 406/5: 34.1.

Argos (map 1): Pisistratus marries Timonassa of, 17.3–4, cf. 19.4; *see also* Pheidon.

Ariphron. Father of Xanthippus: 22.6.

Aristaechmus. Archon 621/0: 4.1.

Aristides: ostracized 483/2, 22.7, *Epit.* 4; partner of Themistocles and founder of Delian League 470s, 23.3–24, *Epit.* 7; but listed as opponent of Themistocles, 28.2; said to foreshadow Ephialtes, 41.2.

Aristion. Proposer of bodyguard for Pisistratus 561/0: 14.1.

Aristocrates. Opponent of Four Hundred: 33.2.

Aristodicus. Of Tanagra; murderer of Ephialtes: 25.4.

Aristogiton. Lover of Harmodius, murderer of Hipparchus I: 18.2–6, cf. (name omitted) *Epit.* 4; his cult, 58.1.

Aristomachus. Chairman at a meeting in 411: 32.1.

Boeotia: legendary king Xanthus, p. 39; constitution, 30.2n.; *see also* Tanagra, Thebes.

Brauron. Home of Pisistratus (map 2):, 13.4n.; *see also* Brauronia, in Glossary.

Bucoleum. Office of *basileus*: 3.5.

Callias I. Archon 412/1: 32.1–2.

Callias II. Archon 406/5: 34.1.

Callibius. Spartan garrison commander sent to Athens 404–403: 37.2, 38.2.

Callicrates. Promises to increase but in fact abolishes two-obol grant in the late fifth century; subsequently condemned to death: 28.3.

Cecrops. Legendary first king of Athens: p. 39.

Index of Persons and Places

Imbros. Aegean island (map 1); settled and ruled from Athens fifth to fourth centuries: 62.2.

Ion. Legendary grandson of king Erechtheus, made polemarch to fight for Athens against Eleusis and Thracians; settles in Athens, divides Athenians into two classes; four tribes named after his sons: pp. 39–40, cf. 3.2, 41.2, *Epit.* 1.

Ionians. Branch of Greek people, said to be descended from Ion: 5.2, cf. p. 40; name used of Athens' allies in Delian League, 23.4–5.

Iophon. Son of Pisistratus: 17.3.

Isagoras. Opponent of Cleisthenes: 20.1–3, cf. 28.2; archon 508/7, 21.1; Spartan attempt to restore him *c.*506, 20.3n.

Laciadae. Deme (map 2): 27.3.

Lemnos. Aegean island (map 1); settled and ruled from Athens fifth to fourth centuries: 61.6, 62.2.

Leocoreum. In Agora (map 3), sanctuary of daughters of Leos; for the *Athenian Constitution*, starting-point of Panathenaic procession: 18.3.

Lesbos. Aegean island (map 1); privileged member of Delian League: 24.2.

Limone. Legendary daughter of Hippomenes, whom he catches in adultery: p. 40, *Epit.* 1.

Lipsydrium. In north Attica (map 2); fortified by Alcmaeonid opponents of Hippias: 19.3.

Lycomedes. Legendary king of Scyros; murders Theseus: p. 39, *Epit.* 1.

Lycurgus. Rival of Pisistratus: 13.4, 14.3, restored to text of 28.2.

Lycus. Legendary son of Pandion: p. 39.

Lygdamis. Of Naxos; supporter of Pisistratus, who makes him tyrant of Naxos: 15.2–3.

Lysander. Spartan admiral: defeats Athens at Aegospotami 405/4; behind installation of Thirty, 34.2–3; sent to support oligarchs 403 but Pausanias sent afterwards, 38.1n.

Lysicrates. Archon 453/2: 26.3.

Lysimachus I. Father of Aristides: 22.7, 23.3.

Lysimachus II. Said to have been saved by Eumelides from council's death sentence: 45.1.

Marathon. Deme (map 2); battle against Persians 490/89: 22.2n., 22.3, 58.1n.

Maronea. In south-east Attica (map 2); rich silver mines yield surplus 483/2: 22.7.

Medon. Legendary king or life archon: 3.3.

Megacles I. Alcmaeonid; archon 630s–620s, responsible for death of Cylon's supporters: p. 41, *Epit.* 2.

Index of Persons and Places

FOR THE BEST IN PAPERBACKS, LOOK FOR THE

In every corner of the world, on every subject under the sun, Penguin represents quality and variety – the very best in publishing today.

For complete information about books available from Penguin – including Pelicans, Puffins, Peregrines and Penguin Classics – and how to order them, write to us at the appropriate address below. Please note that for copyright reasons the selection of books varies from country to country.

In the United Kingdom: For a complete list of books available from Penguin in the U.K., please write to *Dept E.P., Penguin Books Ltd, Harmondsworth, Middlesex, UB7 0DA*

In the United States: For a complete list of books available from Penguin in the U.S., please write to *Dept BA, Penguin, 299 Murray Hill Parkway, East Rutherford, New Jersey 07073*

In Canada: For a complete list of books available from Penguin in Canada, please write to *Penguin Books Canada Ltd, 2801 John Street, Markham, Ontario L3R 1B4*

In Australia: For a complete list of books available from Penguin in Australia, please write to the *Marketing Department, Penguin Books Australia Ltd, P.O. Box 257, Ringwood, Victoria 3134*

In New Zealand: For a complete list of books available from Penguin in New Zealand, please write to the *Marketing Department, Penguin Books (NZ) Ltd, Private Bag, Takapuna, Auckland 9*

In India: For a complete list of books available from Penguin, please write to *Penguin Overseas Ltd, 706 Eros Apartments, 56 Nehru Place, New Delhi, 110019*

In Holland: For a complete list of books available from Penguin in Holland, please write to *Penguin Books Nederland B.V., Postbus 195, NL–1380 AD Weesp, Netherlands*

In Germany: For a complete list of books available from Penguin, please write to *Penguin Books Ltd, Friedrichstrasse 10 – 12, D–6000 Frankfurt Main 1, Federal Republic of Germany*

In Spain: For a complete list of books available from Penguin in Spain, please write to *Longman Penguin España, Calle San Nicolas 15, E–28013 Madrid, Spain*

PENGUIN CLASSICS

AESCHYLUS

Translated by Philip Vellacott

THE ORESTEIAN TRILOGY

What is justice? How is it related to vengeance? Can justice be reconciled with the demands of religion, the violence of human feeling, the forces of Fate?

These questions, which puzzled thoughtful Athenians in the decades after the battle of Marathon, provided the theme for the *Agamemnon*, *The Choephori*, and *The Eumenides*, those grim tragedies that make up the Oresteian Trilogy. In these plays Aeschylus (525–456 B.C.) takes as his subject the bloody character of murder and revenge within the royal family of Argos – a chain finally broken only by the intervention of the goddess Athene. Philip Vellacott's verse translation makes available to the modern reader a milestone in the history of drama.

PROMETHEUS BOUND
AND OTHER PLAYS

Aeschylus (525–456 B.C.) was the first of the great Greek tragedians. The four plays presented in this volume – together with the Oresteian Trilogy – are all that survive of his work. *The Persians* is set against the Athenian victory at Salamis, which took place only eight years before the play was written. In *Seven Against Thebes* the two sons of Oedipus are relentlessly pursued to their death by a family curse. But in *The Suppliants* and *Prometheus* conflict of principle is resolved by rational compromise.

PENGUIN CLASSICS

ARISTOPHANES

LYSISTRATA/THE ACHARNIANS/THE CLOUDS

Translated by Alan H. Sommerstein

Aristophanes (*c.* 450–*c.* 385 B.C.), a contemporary of Socrates, was the last and greatest of the Old Attic Comedians. Only eleven of his plays survive, and this volume contains *Lysistrata*, the hilariously bawdy anti-war fantasy; *The Acharnians*, a plea for peace set against the background of the long war with Sparta, and *The Clouds*, a satire on contemporary philosophy. Writing at a time when Athens was undergoing a crisis in its social attitudes, Aristophanes was an eloquent opponent of the demagogue and the sophist, and his comedy reveals a longing for the return of a peaceful and honest way of life.

THE WASPS/THE POET AND THE WOMEN/THE FROGS

Translated by David Barrett

This collection of Aristophanes' plays contains *The Wasps*, one of his earliest, *The Poet and the Women* (*Thesmophoriazusae*), a gem of parody and low comedy, and *The Frogs*, a comic masterpiece written under the shadow of defeat. A century later the Old Comedy was already thought crude and old-fashioned, yet today much of the humour and fantasy seems oddly contemporary. At the same time Aristophanes has a way of letting the reader right into the spirit of Athens during the long, tragic war against Sparta.

PENGUIN CLASSICS

SOPHOCLES

Translated by E. F. Watling

ELECTRA AND OTHER PLAYS

This volume contains four plays by Sophocles (496–406 B.C.), who was the first to give to ancient Greek drama a structure recognizably related to its modern descendant. In *Electra* he objectively presents part of the Oresteian legend, while *Women of Trachis* is remarkable for the human verisimilitude imparted to a near-repulsive piece of mythology. *Philoctetes* portrays the struggles of right against might, and *Ajax* takes for its theme that of the great man fallen.

THE THEBAN PLAYS

These three plays by Sophocles (496–406 B.C.), thought they are all based on the legend of the royal house of Thebes, were written at different periods and dramatize different themes. *Antigone* is the tragedy of a woman ruled by conscience, an over-confident king, and a young man tormented by conflicting loyalties. *King Oedipus* is a vast and living portrait of a man, without parallel in the Greek theatre, and *Oedipus at Colonus* completes the story with the legend of the passing of the aged hero.

'Mr Watling's translation ... is extremely successful'
– *Journal of Hellenic Studies*

PENGUIN CLASSICS

EURIPIDES

Translated by Philip Vellacott

MEDEA AND OTHER PLAYS

Four plays by Euripides (484–406 B.C.) are presented in this volume in modern English by Philip Vellacott, who has already translated many of the great Greek dramas for the Penguin Classics.

Medea, the story of that princess's horrible revenge for the infidelity of Jason, the hero of the Argonauts, is Euripides' earliest surviving tragedy, whilst *Heracles* is among his latest plays. In *Hecabe* and *Electra* he again underlines the wickedness of revenge. An outspoken critic of society and the gods, Euripides was at his most eloquent on the theme of human suffering, and among the most lyrical of all poets.

ALCESTIS AND OTHER PLAYS

Euripides (484–406 B.C.) is seen in the three plays in this volume as the sceptical questioner of his age. *Alcestis*, an early play in which a queen agrees to die to save her husband's life, is cast in a tragic vein, although it contains passages of satire and even comedy, whilst *Iphigeneia in Tauris*, with its apparently happy ending, melodramatically reunites the ill-fated children of Agamemnon. *Hippolytus*, however, is pure tragedy – the fatal result of Phaedra's unreasoning passion for her chaste stepson. Philip Vellacott's translations, a blend of prose and verse, are designed for the modern stage.

PENGUIN CLASSICS

EURIPIDES

Translated by Philip Vellacott

THE BACCHAE AND OTHER PLAYS

Euripides (484–406 B.C.) is the most modern of the great Greek tragedians, as the four plays in this volume demonstrate. *Ion* is concerned with the problem of reconciling religious faith with the facts of human life, whilst *The Women of Troy* is a plain denunciation of the ruthlessness of war. In *Helen* Euripides light-heartedly parodied himself, and finally, in his last and probably his greatest tragedy, *The Bacchae*, he dealt with mob violence and mass hysteria. Philip Vellacott's fluent translation and valuable introduction make it easier than ever for the modern reader to bridge the two thousand years between himself and these plays.

ORESTES AND OTHER PLAYS

This volume completes the series of Euripides' plays translated for the Penguin Classics by Philip Vellacott. It contains, in chronological order, six plays which span the last twenty-four years of Euripides' career, from the age of fifty to his death in 407 B.C.: *The Children of Heracles, Andromache, The Suppliant Women, The Phoenician Women, Orestes,* and *Iphigenia in Aulis.* The plays differ widely in both form and content; all are ironical in tone; their principal theme is war – the ideals which can redeem it, the guilt which it breeds, the values which it destroys. Expressed in some of Euripides' finest poetic and dramatic writing, these plays form a moral and political statement unique in the ancient world and prophetically relevant in our own.

'Penguin continue to pour out the jewels of the world's classics in translation ... There are now nearly enough to keep a man happy on a desert island until the boat comes in' – Philip Howard in *The Times*

A selection

Chekhov
THE DUEL AND OTHER STORIES
Translated by Ronald Wilks

Marguerite de Navarre
THE HEPTAMERON
Translated by Paul Chilton

Farid ud-Din Attar
THE CONFERENCE OF THE BIRDS
Translated and with an Introduction by
Afkham Darbandi and Dick Davis

Basho
ON LOVE AND BARLEY: THE HAIKU OF BASHO
Translated by Lucien Stryk

THE POEM OF THE CID
Translated by R. Hamilton and J. Perry

Rousseau
DISCOURSE ON THE ORIGINS OF INEQUALITY
Translated by Maurice Cranston